Audi-Dissertationsreihe

EXTERNAL KNOWLEDGE SOURCING FROM STARTUPS:
AN ANALYSIS OF THE PRE-COLLABORATION PHASE

Franz Simon

Graduation Committee:

Chairman and Secretary:
Prof. Dr. Th.A.J. Toonen   University of Twente, BMS

Supervisor:
Prof. Dr. habil. H. Schiele   University of Twente, BMS

Co-Supervisor:
Dr. habil. R. Harms   University of Twente, BMS

Members of the Committee:
Prof. Dr. ir. F.J.A.M. van Houten   University of Twente, ET
Prof. Dr. C.P.M. Wilderom   University of Twente, BMS
Prof. Dr. J. Hallikas   Lappeenranta University of Technology
Prof. Dr. C. Ihl   Technische Universität Hamburg-Harburg
Dr. L. Knight   University of Aston

Bibliografische Information der Deutschen Nationalbibliothek

Die Deutsche Nationalbibliothek verzeichnet diese Publikation in der Deutschen Nationalbibliografie; detaillierte bibliographische Daten sind im Internet über http://dnb.d-nb.de abrufbar.

1. Aufl. - Göttingen: Cuvillier, 2018

© CUVILLIER VERLAG, Göttingen 2018
   Nonnenstieg 8, 37075 Göttingen
   Telefon: 0551-54724-0
   Telefax: 0551-54724-21
   www.cuvillier.de

   ISBN 978-3-7369-9870-4
   eISBN 978-3-7369-8870-5

EXTERNAL KNOWLEDGE SOURCING FROM STARTUPS: AN ANALYSIS OF THE PRE-COLLABORATION PHASE

DISSERTATION

to obtain
the degree of doctor at the University of Twente,
on the authority of the rector magnificus,
prof.dr. T.T.M. Palstra,
on account of the decision of the graduation committee,
to be publicly defended
on Wednesday, October 17, 2018, at 12.45 hrs.

by

Franz Simon

born on February 29, 1988
in Eichstätt, Germany

This dissertation has been approved by:

Prof. Dr. habil. H. Schiele   Supervisor
Dr. habil. R. Harms   Co-supervisor

Table of contents

List of tables

List of figures

List of abbreviations

CL	Construct loading
CVC	Corporate venture capital
H	Hypothesis
ICC	Intraclass correlation
ICT	Information and communications technology
IP	Intellectual property
NPD	New product development
M&A	Mergers and acquisitions
MFL	Method factor loading
KBV	Knowledge-based view
OEM	Original equipment manufacturer
OLS	Ordinary least squares
PLS	Partial least squares
R&D	Research and development
RQ	Research question
SD	Standard deviation
VIF	Variance inflation factor

Chapter 1 – Introduction

Firms increasingly rely on external knowledge. Recently, startups have evolved to an important source of innovation. This dissertation examines how corporations can access knowledge provided by startups. Chapter 1 provides the theoretical background, highlights the research questions that form the core of this dissertation, and introduces the subsequent four chapters (Chapters 2, 3, 4 and 5).

1.1. Motivation and main research question

Digitalization has increasing impact on product-focused industries such as the automotive industry (Nambisan, 2017; Svahn, Mathiassen, & Lindgren, 2017). The resulting turbulences have forced corporations to respond to emerging technological developments as well as changes in their market environments (Bergek, Berggren, Magnusson, & Hobday, 2013). To remain competitive in such environments, firms need to explore new technological paths and access external knowledge as an extension to internal innovation activities (Criscuolo, Laursen, Reichstein, & Salter, 2018; Laursen & Salter, 2006; Leiponen & Helfat, 2010; Rosenkopf & Nerkar, 2001). External knowledge adds new variations of problem solutions that are unknown to the in-sourcing organization (Fleming & Sorenson, 2001; Katila & Ahuja, 2002; March, 1991). By combining external knowledge with existing routines, firms generate new knowledge (Zollo & Winter, 2002). Thus, continuous creative stimuli from their environment enable firms to generate radically new solutions and to build own innovation capabilities (Colombo, von Krogh, Rossi-Lamastra, & Stephan, 2017; Kogut & Zander, 1992).

Collaborations with customers, suppliers, universities, or even competitors are a promising way to extend the own knowledge base (Van de Vrande, 2013; West & Bogers, 2014). Suppliers have large impact on product innovation, but the knowledge corporate firms need to access cannot always be found within the existing networks of their organizations (Brusoni, Prencipe, & Pavitt, 2001; Schiele, 2006; Un, Cuervo-Cazurra, & Asakawa, 2010). Recently, startups as new knowledge providers have received growing attention (Monteiro & Birkinshaw, 2017; Weiblen & Chesbrough, 2015; Zaremba, Bode, & Wagner, 2017). By engaging in partnerships with startups, firms aim to benefit from startups' entrepreneurial characteristics and knowledge (Audretsch, Segarra, & Teruel, 2014; Criscuolo, Nicolaou, & Salter, 2012; Marion, Friar, & Simpson, 2012).

Startups are newly founded firms younger than six to eight years (Song, Podoynitsyna, Van Der Bij, & Halman, 2008) and are mainly defined by their liability of newness (Stinchcombe, 1965). According to Singh, Tucker, and House (1986, p. 171), "[t]his liability of newness occurs because young organizations have to learn new roles as social actors, coordinate new roles for employees and deal with problems of mutual socialization of participants, and because of both their inability to compete effectively with established organizations and their low levels of legitimacy." As startups miss assets, they cannot experiment with many different ideas, but have to focus on specific ones (van Burg, Podoynitsyna, Beck, & Lommelen, 2012). Thus, new product development (NPD) is more focused and dynamic within startups compared to established organizations (Rothaermel, 2002). Further, startups apply customer-centric methods like "design thinking" or "lean startup", which allow early interaction as well as continuous iterations with customers (Blank, 2013; Weiblen & Chesbrough, 2015). Innovation capabilities are vital for startups to quickly access market shares and early cash flows (Schoonhoven, Eisenhardt, & Lyman, 1990). Due to small firm size, startups can sustain high flexibility and short chains of command (Kickul, Griffiths, Jayaram, & Wagner, 2011; Rothaermel, 2002). Finally, startups possess high willingness to take risks and high growth potential which allows to accomplish a prime position for innovation, especially radical innovation (Criscuolo et al., 2012; Engel, 2011). Overall, startups show distinct differences to established organizations (Brunswicker & Hutschek, 2010; Gassmann, Zeschky, Wolff, & Stahl, 2010).

Prior research has focused on how firms can access knowledge form their established suppliers by screening their supply base (Johnsen, 2009; Pulles, Veldman, & Schiele, 2014; Schiele, 2006). In a consecutive step, firms try to achieve a prime position to access supplier knowledge as they aim to become their preferred customer (Hüttinger, Schiele, & Schröer, 2014; Pulles, Schiele, Veldman, & Hüttinger, 2016; Schiele, 2012; Steinle & Schiele, 2008). Yet, the literature misses an analysis on how to access knowledge beyond the established supply base such as knowledge originating startups (Weiblen & Chesbrough, 2015; Zaremba et al., 2017). Concerning the impact of knowledge provided by startups, existing studies show that incorporating their knowledge increases the innovation performance of corporations (Dushnitsky & Lenox, 2006; Wadhwa, Phelps, & Kotha, 2016). Although organizations theory shows that firms rely on external stimuli in their knowledge generation process (Agarwal & Helfat, 2009; Eisenhardt & Martin, 2000), no existing study has considered the effects of implementing structured search for startups. As a consequence, this dissertation focuses on the following primary research question:

Which approaches do corporations follow to access knowledge provided by startups and what are the implications on the organization?

In sum, startups have evolved to an important source of innovation. As it may become essential for corporations to identify knowledge originating startups and to become an attractive partner for startups, this dissertation focuses on the pre-collaboration phase of corporate-startup relationships. The pre-collaboration phase concerns all activities before engaging in collaborative work or signing formal agreements. Therefore, the present work focuses mainly on the identification of partners and also considers what decides about whether or not firms enter into corporate-startup collaborations.

1.2. Theoretical background

This dissertation builds on external knowledge sourcing literature. External knowledge sourcing is defined as the firms' ability to *"tap into new ideas and technologies from beyond their boundaries"* (Monteiro & Birkinshaw, 2017, p. 342). Thereby, organizations identify new solutions by creating and recombining knowledge across boundaries (Katila & Ahuja, 2002; Rosenkopf & Nerkar, 2001).

Extensive research provides evidence for the positive relationship between openness to external knowledge and firms' innovation performance (Lakemond, Bengtsson, Laursen, & Tell, 2016; Laursen & Salter, 2006; Leiponen & Helfat, 2010; van Wijk, Jansen, & Lyles, 2008; Wadhwa et al., 2016). In addition, the acquisition and application of external knowledge contributes to firms' renewal and extension of their capabilities (Agarwal & Helfat, 2009; Eisenhardt & Martin, 2000). Besides underlining the value of distinct knowledge providers (e.g., suppliers, customers, or universities), the literature has introduced different approaches to access external knowledge. The external sourcing continuum ranges from acquisitions (Ahuja & Katila, 2001; Andersson & Xiao, 2016) and minority investments (Dushnitsky & Lenox, 2006; Wadhwa & Basu, 2013) to strategic alliances (Lavie, 2007; Stuart, 2000).

Theoretically, external knowledge sourcing is closely linked to the knowledge-based view (KBV) of the firm (Grant, 1996b; March, 1991). According to the KBV, knowledge is considered as the most important firm resource (Grant, 1996b; Nickerson & Zenger, 2004; Nonaka, 1994). Hence, firms' existence is primarily grounded on coordinating mechanisms to integrate specialized knowledge (Grant, 1996a; Kogut & Zander, 1992). Further, the KBV claims that "the heterogeneous knowledge bases and capabilities among firms are the main determinants of performance differences" (DeCarolis & Deeds, 1999, p. 954). In other words, the firms' ability to explore, acquire, retain, integrate, and exploit knowledge is central to firms value creation (Grant, 1996b). This is especially valid in knowledge-intensive contexts, such as the high-technology sectors (Bingham & Davis, 2012; Steensma & Corley, 2000).

Especially, startups as an external source of knowledge positively impact the sourcing organizations' innovation performance (Benson & Ziedonis, 2009; Dushnitsky & Lenox, 2006). In order to access knowledge provided by startups, corporations have to consider their specific needs based on missing organizational routines (Minshall, Mortara, Elia, & Probert, 2008; Minshall, Mortara, Valli, & Probert, 2010; Prashantham & Birkinshaw, 2008). From the perspective of startups, collaborations with corporations imply tensions between value creation and knowledge misappropriation (Diestre & Rajagopalan, 2012; Katila, Rosenberger, & Eisenhardt, 2008). With much more power in the collaboration, corporations can even endanger the survival of startups. Still, smaller firms also benefit from partnerships with corporations as they can access new markets and technologies (H. Chen & Chen, 2002; Kalaignanam, Shankar, & Varadarajan, 2007).

1.3. Focus of this research and methodology

With focus on the pre-collaboration phase of relationships between corporations and startups, this dissertation applies an input-process-output model to study the identification and access of knowledge provided by startups (see Figure 1). "Input" is defined by specific criteria that are inherent to startup and corporate organizations. "Process" describes how organizations interact prior to setting up a collaboration and which organizational approaches are implemented. Finally, "output" defines the implications of initiating corporate-startups collaborations, e.g., organizational learning for the corporation and feedback or reputation for startups.

From the perspective of the sourcing corporation, the quality of startups ideas serves as the "input" for decisions on whether to engage in partnerships with startups and if these relations have the potential to be value-adding for the organization. Consequently, chapter 2 examines the quality of startup ideas. Chapter 3 and 4 show how corporations organize the search for startups and which search strategies are followed. Accordingly, these chapters focus on the "process" of establishing such collaborations. Taking the perspective of startups, chapter 5 investigates how corporations may become attractive partners for startups. By considering resources and assets that can be provided by corporations and taking relational aspects into account, this chapter contributes to all three phases. The following sub-chapters introduce the motivation and background of each chapter, as well as the proposed research questions and methodological approaches.

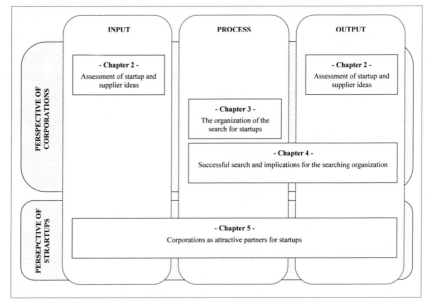

Figure 1: Dissertation outline by an input-process-output model

1.3.1. Assessment of startup and supplier ideas

Suppliers have been broadly regarded as the most influential external partner providing positive effects for a firms' innovative output (Al-Zu'bi & Tsinopoulos, 2012; Lau, Tang, & Yam, 2010; Un et al., 2010; Wagner, 2012; Yeniyurt, Henke Jr, & Yalcinkaya, 2014). Yet, not all innovation efforts with suppliers are successful (Koufteros, Vonderembse, & Jayaram, 2005; Song & Thieme, 2009). Thus, firms have begun to tap beyond their established supply base and have started to look for new partners such as startups (Weiblen & Chesbrough, 2015; Zaremba, Bode, & Wagner, 2016; Zaremba et al., 2017). While there are studies on how to integrate startups into the existing supply base (Zaremba et al., 2017) or collaborate in programs (Bergek & Norrman, 2008; Pauwels, Clarysse, Wright, & Van Hove, 2016), an examining how startups actually perform as an external source of innovation misses. Especially, no prior study has investigated the performance of startups in comparison to suppliers in a real-world empirical setting. This is an important research gap as in the long run the results will guide a firm's decision whether or not to invest in the collaboration with startups, which typically involve more effort and uncertainty compared to relationships with established suppliers. Consequently, the first research question (RQ1) is: *How do startups and established suppliers perform compared to each other in generating promising innovation ideas?*

To empirically examine this research question, a global automotive firm provided a dataset with 314 supplier and startups ideas containing idea assessments and longitudinal information regarding the implementation of these ideas. Hence, we were able to draw on unique data and investigate our research question under real-word conditions in a naturalistic setting, which is similar to existing studies exploring the quality of innovation ideas (e.g., Björk & Magnusson, 2009; Lilien, Morrison, Searls, Sonnack, & Hippel, 2002). We used ordinary least squares (OLS) and binary logistic regression to investigate the differences in idea quality and implementation among supplier and startup ideas. In addition, we applied quantile regression for further analysis.

1.3.2. The organization of the search for startups

Search as a strategic task has been regarded from various angles within open innovation literature (Gavetti & Levinthal, 2000; Knudsen & Srikanth, 2014; Lopez-Vega, Tell, & Vanhaverbeke, 2016). Existing studies have investigated the identification of various external knowledge partners, e.g., applying competitions for suppliers in the early stages of firms' innovation processes (Langner & Seidel, 2009). In particular, scholars have so far focused on how corporations identify innovative partners within their supply base (Pulles et al., 2014; Schiele, 2006). Regarding the identification of new partners such as startups, the literature is limited to very specific approaches that focus on the establishment of external scouting units (Gassmann & Gaso, 2004; Monteiro & Birkinshaw, 2017). Yet, the literature misses a holistic analysis on how to identify innovative partners beyond established networks. Therefore, the following research question (RQ2) is introduced: *Which approaches do corporations apply to search for startups?*

To investigate this research question, we applied a multiple case study among eight automotive corporations. Following a key informant approach we interviewed 13 employees from innovation management, research and development (R&D), procurement, mergers and acquisitions (M&A), strategy, and corporate venture capital (CVC) (John & Reve, 1982). The data from the interviews were enriched by accessing publicly available materials, e.g., articles, Crunchbase, CB Insights and company websites. For the data analysis, we followed a structured approach that included: transcribing all interview data, coding, discussing codes with peers, and continuously reviewing of all interview transcripts and secondary data.

1.3.3. Search strategies for startups and the implications for the searching organization

All prior studies concerning the search for startups are qualitative and describe only selected search approaches (Homfeldt, Rese, Brenner, Baier, & Schäfer, 2017; Weiblen & Chesbrough, 2015). As an extension to study 2, the following part analyzes which search strategies are most successful for the identification of startups. Moreover, prior research points out that corporate organizations often under-invest in the realization of truly novel ideas (Henderson, 1993), because these mature organizations face inertia routed in their organizational routines (Levinthal & March, 1993), structures (O'Connor & Rice, 2013), and mental models (Tripsas & Gavetti, 2000). By accessing knowledge from startups, firms aim at overcoming this myopia and increase their innovation performance (Wadhwa et al., 2016). Thereby, scholars have primarily focused on collaborations with startups in form of minority investments (Dushnitsky & Lenox, 2006) or joint development projects (Gassmann et al., 2010). No existing study has analyzed the effects of implementing structured search for startups, although the generation of new knowledge requires the integration of external stimuli (Zollo & Winter, 2002). This study proposes that the search for startups implies necessary external impulses to generate radical innovations and subsequently expands the firms' organizational capabilities. Hence, the third research question (RQ3) addresses both described gaps: *How do corporations achieve successful search for startups to enhance their organizational capabilities?*

To answer this research question and to test our hypotheses on a profound empirical basis, we surveyed a cross-industry sample by means of a self-administered internet-based survey. The final dataset consisted of 97 firms. We operationalized search strategy with the commonly applied constructs for search breadth and search depths (Laursen & Salter, 2006, 2014; Leiponen & Helfat, 2010). In contrary to analyzing knowledge sources, we examined the application of eleven search instruments (e.g., startup pitch events or databases). OLS and polynomial regression allowed to analyze the introduced model.

1.3.4. Corporations as attractive partners for startups

Prior research has neglected the perspective of firms providing external knowledge (Monteiro, Mol, & Birkinshaw, 2017; Rothaermel & Alexandre, 2009). Especially, the perspective of startups has not received sufficient attention yet (Alvarez & Barney, 2001; Katila et al., 2008). On the one hand, corporations can assist startups to overcome constraints concerning their liability of newness (Stuart, 2000; Stuart, Hoang, & Hybels, 1999) or missing technological capabilities (Andersson & Xiao, 2016; Mitchell & Singh, 1992). On the other hand, startups may be confronted with risks, such as dependency or misappropriation of intellectual property (IP) (Diestre & Rajagopalan, 2012; Katila et al., 2008). Still, benefits and risks of corporate-startup collaborations have been considered only isolated and the literature lacks an analysis how entrepreneurs weight such factors when it comes to establishing their willingness to collaborate. Therefore, the fourth study regards the following research question (RQ4): *Which factors influence the willingness of startups to enter collaborations with corporations?*

Building on a sample of twelve startups, we were able to analyze 30 corporate-startup collaborations within our cases. The sample consists of startups with established relations to corporations and startups without experiences concerning collaborations. Further, the selected cases belong to different industries, e.g., information and communications technology (ICT) or manufacturing, and differ according to the development stage of their technology. To facilitate triangulation, we included both, interview and secondary data. All interviews were transcribed and coded. We followed a multiple-step approach to cluster and analyze our data, as proposed by Gioia, Corley, and Hamilton (2013).

1.4. Research outline and contributions

In sum, this dissertation consists of four articles that contribute to a better understanding of the pre-collaboration phase of relationships between startups and corporations. In doing so, we add primarily to literature on external knowledge sourcing. Starting with the perspective of corporations, chapter 2 examines the quality of startup ideas. The subsequent chapters deal with the search for startups and its implications on the searching organization. Finally, chapter 5 respects the perspective of startups by highlighting how corporations may evolve to attractive partners for startups. Figure 2 illustrates the structure of the present dissertation. The following paragraphs summarize the contributions per chapter.

Chapter 2 compares ideas from suppliers and startups, which were identified, evaluated, and followed up in the course of an open innovation initiative conducted within a large automotive manufacturer. The evaluation of the ideas contains the degree of novelty, customer benefit, and implementation. Therefore, this part of the dissertation adds new dimensions to the discourse on open innovation and external knowledge sourcing. Moreover, contributions to the growing stream of research focusing on external knowledge provided by startups can be made (Monteiro & Birkinshaw, 2017; Weiblen & Chesbrough, 2015). The findings shed light on the question if startups are more promising innovation partners than existing suppliers. Hence, we answer the question whether it really matters for corporations to engage in collaborations with startups.

Chapter 3 focuses on the search for external knowledge, which has evolved to a major strategic task for corporations. More specifically, this part analyzes how corporations search for startups and therefore regards which organizational approaches and processes are installed as well as which search instruments corporations apply to support their search for startups. The findings of this study add to literature on external knowledge sourcing by illustrating how firms search for knowledge outside their networks. Thus, an important gap in literature can be addressed since prior studies have exclusively focused on the identification of innovative partners within existing networks (Pulles et al., 2014; Schiele, 2006). In addition, several organizational structures are identified that allow corporate organizations to realize boundary spanning to access knowledge provided by startups (Rosenkopf & Almeida, 2003; Rosenkopf & Nerkar, 2001).

Chapter 4 provides an analysis of search strategies for the successful identification of startups and highlights the effects of these search activities on the searching firms' organizational capabilities. As a first step, the effects of open search breadth and search depth on the success of search for startups are investigated. Similar approaches to measure search breadth and depth have been applied in open innovation literature before (Criscuolo et al., 2018; Laursen & Salter, 2006; Monteiro et al., 2017). Second, this study investigates whether the search for startups provides stimuli to enhance the searching firms' radical innovation capabilities and consequently the firms' organizational capabilities (Colombo et al., 2017; Zollo & Winter, 2002). It is further investigated if distant knowledge, which is inherent in startups, provides additional new variations of knowledge and explorative ideas to solve existing problems for corporations (Fleming & Sorenson, 2004; Katila & Ahuja, 2002; March, 1991). By showing that the discovery of promising startups and the assessment of their ideas provide creative stimuli for the sourcing organization, an important gap in literature regarding the effects of search on organizational capabilities is addressed (Colombo et al., 2017; O'Connor & De Martino, 2006; Zollo & Winter, 2002).

Chapter 5 illuminates the perspective of startups in corporate-startups relationships. In doing so, this part of the dissertation focuses the prospect of external knowledge providers, which has been underrepresented in prior research (Monteiro & Birkinshaw, 2017; Rothaermel & Alexandre, 2009). The study investigates how complementary assets provided by corporations as well as risks and relational characteristics influence startups' decisions on engaging in corporate-startup collaborations. To achieve a more differentiated perspective, startups are distinguished by the maturity of their technology in early-stage and market-ready. This chapter follows the rising interest in research on collaborations between small firms and larger organizations and in particular on approaches to attract resources of a partnering firm (Street & Cameron, 2007; Yang, Zheng, & Zhao, 2014). Further, the findings illustrate paths to enhance the attractiveness of corporations as partners for startups, which has been previously studied in the field of buyer-supplier relationships (Pulles et al., 2016; Schiele, Veldman, & Hüttinger, 2011).

Figure 2: Structure of the dissertation

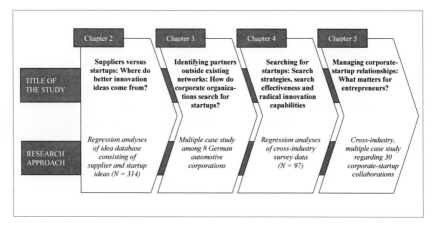

Chapter 2 – Suppliers versus startups: Where do better innovation ideas come from?

Abstract

Suppliers increasingly play a key role as external sources of ideas in the innovation process of firms. While the beneficial impact of supplier integration is generally acknowledged, there is also evidence that not all such innovation efforts are successful, particularly concerning the identification of truly innovative solutions. In recent years, many firms have therefore begun to tap beyond their existing supply base and increasingly draw on ideas from startups–yet, there is no empirical evidence whether their ideas really outperform those of established suppliers. We address this open question by presenting a unique real-world comparison of 314 supplier and startup ideas identified, evaluated, and followed up in the course of an open innovation initiative conducted within a large automotive manufacturer. We find that startup ideas are indeed characterized by a higher degree of novelty and customer benefit, but, on the downside, are less likely to be implemented than supplier ideas. However, the implemented startup ideas in our sample are still more novel. Overall, our study adds new dimensions to the discourse on open innovation and provides valuable insights regarding the outcome of the involvement of suppliers and startups in the front end of the innovation process.

2.1. Introduction

In today's dynamic marketplace, ever demanding customer needs for new products requires firms to constantly innovate in order to sustain competiveness. Because ideas are precursors to innovations (George, 2007), firms are relying on a continuous stream of ideas into the front end of their NPD process where ideation typically takes place (Björk & Magnusson, 2009; Kim & Wilemon, 2002). While internal R&D experts have long been seen as a sufficient source of innovation ideas, there is today a broad consensus that a key driver of a firm's innovation success is external knowledge sourcing, that is, the search for and use of new ideas and technologies from partners outside the firm (Chesbrough, 2003; Laursen & Salter, 2006).

Considering the potential set of external partners, such as established suppliers, users, or universities, suppliers seem to have the largest impact on product innovation (Un et al., 2010). Extensive research exists on supplier involvement in NPD, providing evidence that partnering with suppliers positively affects a firm's innovative output (e.g., Al-Zu'bi & Tsinopoulos, 2012; Lau et al., 2010; Wagner, 2012; Yeniyurt et al., 2014). However, there is also evidence that not all innovation efforts with suppliers are successful. For instance, Song and Thieme (2009) reveal that market intelligence gathering with suppliers in predesign tasks is negatively related to product performance in radical innovation projects. Koufteros et al. (2005) also find negative effects of supplier integration but on a firm's product innovation capability. Similarly, Gassmann et al. (2010) report in their case study with BMW that established suppliers failed to propose truly innovative ideas that met the expectations of the car manufacturer.

It is thus not surprising that firms have begun to tap beyond their established supply base looking for new partners and increasingly rely on new ventures, that are, young (i.e., eight years old or younger) firms without a preexisting business relation to the buying firm, commonly labeled as "startups" (Homfeldt et al., 2017; Monteiro & Birkinshaw, 2017; Weiblen & Chesbrough, 2015; Zaremba et al., 2016, 2017). Compared to established suppliers, startups are more dynamic and flexible. Startups are seen as a source of truly innovative ideas with the ability to respond quickly to disruptive technological changes (Christensen & Bower, 1996). Overall, the innovative potential of startups "stands out as a highly attractive feature" (Zaremba et al., 2016, p. 153), making them interesting innovation partners for buying firms. Vice versa, entering into partnerships with reputed firms is crucial for startup survival, because these firms confer access to needed resources and help startups to gain the required market access for their ideas (Santos & Eisenhardt, 2009; Stuart et al., 1999).

Accordingly, academia has emphasized important research directions at the interface between entrepreneurship and innovation-oriented disciplines (Ireland & Webb, 2007), highlighting the use of startups in the early stages of a firm's innovation process (Kickul et al., 2011). While scholars have started to investigate how firms search for startups (Monteiro & Birkinshaw, 2017) and integrate them into their existing supply base (Zaremba et al., 2017), an examination of how startups actually perform as a source of innovation ideas has been missing so far. Moreover, the existing literature does not take the open innovation scenario into account that a firm has specific innovation needs and addresses these needs both to startups and its established suppliers with the aim to identify promising ideas. Thus, a real-world empirical comparison of ideas generated by suppliers and startups has not yet been carried out. This is an important research gap because in the long run the results will guide a firm's decision whether or not to invest in the collaboration with startups, which typically involve more effort and uncertainty compared to relationships with established suppliers. Consequently, the research question of this study is: *How do established suppliers and startups perform compared to each other in generating promising innovation ideas?*

To answer this question, we present a study that compares 314 supplier and startup ideas in terms of key quality dimensions. All ideas were identified and evaluated in the course of an open innovation initiative conducted within the large German automotive manufacturer AUDI AG. Both suppliers from the existing supply base of the automotive manufacturer as well as non-established, young startup firms were invited to present their ideas based on relevant innovation search fields. Each idea was evaluated in terms of novelty and its benefit for end customers, succeeded by a decision on each idea regarding its implementation.

Overall, our study adds new dimensions to the discourse on open innovation and external knowledge sourcing. We contribute to the growing stream of research on the use of startups as external sources of ideas (Monteiro & Birkinshaw, 2017; Weiblen & Chesbrough, 2015) and pursue the question whether startups really constitute (more) promising innovation partners (than existing suppliers) from the perspective of a buying firm. At the same time, we shed more light on the involvement and outcome of suppliers in the front end of the NPD process, an area that is left largely unexplored (Schoenherr & Wagner, 2016; Wowak, Craighead, Ketchen, & Hult, 2016). While the existing innovation literature concentrates solely on comparing the quality of ideas generated by different user types (Lilien et al., 2002; Magnusson, 2009; Poetz & Schreier, 2012; Schweisfurth, 2017), our study is the first to consider suppliers and startups as increasingly important open innovation partners.

2.2. Theoretical background and hypotheses

2.2.1. Open innovation and the value of external knowledge

A central part of a firm's innovation process is the search for ideas and knowledge with innovative potential (Laursen, 2012). According to Katila and Ahuja (2002, p. 1184), an organization's search process can be defined as "problem-solving activities that involve the creation and recombination of technological ideas". Part of this search relates to the idea potential of the own R&D experts, but this internal knowledge constitutes only one element. More importantly, since essential knowledge often resides outside the own boundary (Powell, Koput, & Smith-Doerr, 1996), firms are required to tap into external knowledge in order to find novel and useful ideas (Salter, Wal, Criscuolo, & Alexy, 2015). Especially over the last two decades, studies of how firms identify and benefit from external knowledge have increased considerably in particular due to the publicity enjoyed by the open innovation paradigm (Bogers et al., 2017; Chesbrough, 2003; Dahlander & Gann, 2010; Randhawa, Wilden, & Hohberger, 2016; West & Bogers, 2014). While internal knowledge often lacks sufficient creative potential and variety (Fleming & Sorenson, 2001; Rosenkopf & Nerkar, 2001), external knowledge increases the potential to achieve high levels of ideation (Salter et al., 2015). Cassiman and Veugelers (2006) confirm that firms only engaging in internal R&D activities tend to have lower innovation performance than firms that combined internal and external sourcing. The positive impact of external knowledge sourcing has been demonstrated by numerous empirical studies (e.g., Y. Chen, Vanhaverbeke, & Du, 2016; Leiponen & Helfat, 2010; Monteiro et al., 2017) and it is against this background that firms have increasingly implemented the concept of open innovation by means of searching for ideas from external partners and using these ideas in their innovation processes (Laursen & Salter, 2006).

2.2.2. Suppliers and startups as external sources of ideas for innovation

Among external sources of knowledge, the crucial role of suppliers in NPD is generally acknowledged (Brusoni et al., 2001; Cabigiosu, Zirpoli, & Camuffo, 2013).While early research on supplier involvement in NPD has primarily focused on related benefits in terms of development speed, product quality, and costs (Clark, 1989; Ragatz, Handfield, & Scannell, 1997), more recent studies have increasingly highlighted the role of suppliers as external sources of innovation. According to Von Hippel (2005), suppliers are, beside users, the major sources of innovation ideas. Rese, Sänn, and Homfeldt (2015) provide some evidence in the automotive sector and show that automotive manufacturers rated the number of innovative ideas from their suppliers significantly highest in comparison to other sources. Un et al. (2010, p. 678) argue that cooperating with suppliers is advantageous for product innovation because their knowledge "is part of a specialized set of skills possessed by the supplier and not the focal firm". Consequently, collaborating with suppliers can help a firm gain new competencies (Wynstra, Van Weele, & Weggemann, 2001), which in turn can contribute to the development of innovative products.

Consistent with these arguments, empirical studies have shown supplier involvement in NPD to be positively related to a firm's innovative output. For instance, Lau et al. (2010) find that product co-development with suppliers is positively associated with product innovativeness in terms of newness to the firm, customer, and industry. Al-Zu'bi and Tsinopoulos (2012) reveal a positive impact of supplier collaboration on product variety, that is, the ability to offer a range of new products and features. Furthermore, Luzzini, Amann, Caniato, Essig, and Ronchi (2015) show that a greater effort on supplier collaboration positively influences a firm's innovation performance, defined as the level of innovation in products and supplier time-to-market for new products. While the vast majority of research examines the involvement and subsequent impact of suppliers in NPD as a whole, Wagner (2012) is the first to explicitly consider the involvement of suppliers in the front end of the NPD process where ideas are typically identified and generated. The results indicate a positive relationship with NPD project performance, thus stressing the need of involving suppliers right from the early stage.

Despite a number of positive examples, however, not all studies agree with the findings of positive innovation returns on supplier involvement in NPD. For instance, Koufteros et al. (2005) find that supplier integration has a negative influence on a firm's ability of developing new and unique products and features. To protect the value of their own knowledge and skills, suppliers might be rather selective in delivering promising ideas to a buying firm, thus preventing the manufacturer from developing really new products (Lau et al., 2010). Several scholars hence argue that established supplier partnerships have limited innovation potential. In particular with regard to the identification of truly innovative solutions, the literature suggests that new competencies and technological ideas from beyond the existing supply base are needed (Gassmann et al., 2010; Phillips, Lamming, Bessant, & Noke, 2006; Primo & Amundson, 2002).

Startups might provide such competencies and ideas. Startups, also referred to as "new ventures", are firms that have not been in existence for a long time. Empirically, it is difficult to determine the maximum age of startups as different cut-off values exist in the literature.

However, even though different age ranges have been used, there is an established consensus that firms eight years old or younger are considered as startups (McDougall, Covin, Robinson, & Herron, 1994; Song et al., 2008; Zahra, 1996). In this study we follow this classification and define startups as firms with a maximum age of eight years and, in further contrast to established suppliers, without a pre-existing business relationship to the respective buying firm.

From a theoretical perspective, startups are characterized by the liability of newness. According to Singh et al. (1986, p. 171), "[t]his liability of newness occurs because young organizations have to learn new roles as social actors, coordinate new roles for employees and deal with problems of mutual socialization of participants, and because of both their inability to compete effectively with established organizations and their low levels of legitimacy." Originating from the liability of newness, startups differ from established (supplier) firms in several aspects. Startups possess fewer resources, less manufacturing capabilities, have less degree of organizational formalization, and lack the legitimacy in the marketplace (Aldrich & Ruef, 2006; Singh et al., 1986; Terjesen, Patel, & Covin, 2011). Because reputed buying firms can provide valuable inputs that compensate for these liabilities, startups have a clear incentive to enter into partnerships with such firms (Zaremba et al., 2017).

Despite the liabilities they face, startups feature several strengths in particular with regard to their innovative abilities. Several scholars stress the innovative potential of startups due to their endowment with entrepreneurial capabilities, such as alertness, creativity, flexibility, and willingness to take risks (Ward, 2004; Weiblen & Chesbrough, 2015). Overall, the ability to innovate is a crucial variable for startup performance (Chrisman, Bauerschmidt, & Hofer, 1998) and essential for gaining external visibility as well as accessing market shares to sustain survival (Schoonhoven et al., 1990). To put it in more straightforward terms, "innovation may be a matter of life or death" for startups (Criscuolo et al., 2012, p. 320). As startups face resource constraints, they are on the one hand limited in experimentation with various new ideas because they cannot afford to develop multiple technologies (van Burg et al., 2012). On the other hand, these constraints boost creativity in idea generation because entrepreneurs are required to be more imaginatively when employing their resources (Baker & Nelson, 2005).

Overall, these attributes illustrate the tremendous innovative potential of startups and it is against this background that firms have begun to extensively draw on technological ideas from startups in addition to or instead of their established suppliers, including the establishment of a variety of ways to engage with startups, such as incubators, accelerators, or other approaches (Homfeldt et al., 2017; Monteiro & Birkinshaw, 2017; Weiblen & Chesbrough, 2015; Zaremba et al., 2017). However, what has been missing so far is an examination of how startups actually perform as a source of innovation ideas in comparison to established suppliers. Addressing this question is important because it simply demonstrates whether it is worth to invest time and resources for the identification of and collaboration with startups, which generally involve more effort compared to established suppliers.

2.2.3. Hypotheses

The creativity literature suggests various dimensions to assess the quality of an idea; though, there are no uniformly applied dimensions and the final choice depends on the context (Magnusson, 2009). However, what is undisputed is that a key distinguishing feature of a promising idea is novelty, that is, the extent to which the idea is original and thus different from solutions available in the market (Amabile, Conti, Coon, Lazenby, & Herron, 1996; Franke, Poetz, & Schreier, 2014). Reflecting on this point, it is widely argued that entrepreneurship embodies the process through which newness is created (Ireland & Webb, 2007). As emphasized before, the innovative behavior of startups is driven by limited resources originating from their liability of newness (Singh et al., 1986). While resource constraints restricts startups in their ability to experiment with multiple ideas and technologies, they in turn spur creativity in idea generation. The underlying mechanism of "bounded creativity" predicts that individuals will produce more original solutions when restrictions apply (Moreau & Dahl, 2005). Facing resource constraints, entrepreneurs are required to break away from conventional ways of ideation and appear to be very resourceful when using their rare resources, thus creating novel solutions (Baker & Nelson, 2005). Startups can use their resources creatively because they do not follow dedicated routines that often represents a barrier to innovation. Instead of having already established structures as they exist in established supplier firms, startup processes are nascent and yield novel outcomes (Baker, Miner, & Eesley, 2003; Katila & Shane, 2005).

Research on creative performance reveals that individuals and organizations are constrained by their past experience in generating ideas, that is, they stick to schemes and strategies that have been successful in the past, thus preventing them from coming up with truly novel solutions (Audia & Goncalo, 2007). According to March (1991), the experience of success induces a shift from exploring new ideas to exploiting existing solutions because the exploitation of existing knowledge that has proven to be successful guarantees more certain results for an organization. Considering their missing product history, startups lack this experience and do not stick to old technological paradigms (Anderson & Tushman, 1990). In contrast, established suppliers usually draw on long-lasting business relations and the breadth of new knowledge that a buying firm can gain for innovation may be rather limited (Un et al., 2010). For instance, Gassmann et al. (2010) illustrate in their case study with BMW how the automotive manufacturer screened its established supply base for innovative ideas for a new control concept solution. The authors find that "[d]espite its suppliers' vast technological know-how and competence in technology integration, they could only come up with proposals that continued the contemporary trend towards 'electronifying' cars' mechanical functions" (Gassmann et al., 2010, p. 645). Song and Thieme (2009) further reveal that market intelligence gathering with suppliers in predesign tasks is positively related to success in incremental innovation projects but negatively in radical innovation projects. Overall, while the literature acknowledges the potential of suppliers to generate novel solutions from the perspective of the buying firm (as it is shown by our literature review in the previous section), we expect that startups perform better in direct comparison. Hence, based on the overall discussion, we hypothesize that:

Hypothesis 1:　　　*Ideas generated by startups are characterized by a higher degree of novelty than ideas generated by suppliers.*

Researchers studying innovation highlight that novelty of an idea or solution is only one of the two conceptual elements of successful innovation. Accordingly, an idea must also be useful, that is, it has to meet a certain need and create benefits for a potentially large number of end consumers (Amabile et al., 1996; Franke et al., 2014; Moreau & Dahl, 2005). To sustain survival, startups need not only generate novel but also useful ideas that will appeal to some identifiable market (Ward, 2004). By founding a firm, startups align their entrepreneurial activities with such identified market opportunities (Alvarez & Barney, 2004). Discovering promising opportunities at an early stage when potential consumers develop interest for new solutions is seen as an inherent capability of startups (Ireland, Hitt, & Sirmon, 2003). Idea generation within startups thus can be described as not only resourceful but also "necessity-driven" (van Burg et al., 2012). In so doing, startups apply methods, such as design thinking or the principle "lean startup" in order to support early interaction with end consumers. Through iterative testing of their ideas on the market, startups receive continuous feedback, which allows them to develop solutions that provide benefits to potential users (Blank, 2013; Ries, 2011). Due to their position at the edge of developments in a specific domain, startups perceive real-world needs and problems early and can generate solutions to these needs. In turn, established firms such as suppliers commonly focus on improving their existing solutions, which often result in failure of satisfying consumer needs (Christensen & Bower, 1996; Ireland et al., 2003). Therefore, we propose that:

Hypothesis 2:   *Ideas generated by startups are characterized by a higher degree of customer benefit than ideas generated by suppliers.*

Beside the two distinguishing attributes of novelty and customer benefit, creativity alone is not enough and the ultimate proof of an idea's quality can be seen in its implementation by a company (thus serving as a holistic quality measure), which is particularly important to consider in the industrial context where many ideas fail to be implemented, e.g., because they are not technically and/or economically feasible or possess less organizational fit (Lilien et al., 2002; Poetz & Schreier, 2012). Levitt (1963, p. 79) already stated that "[i]deas are useless unless used".

In recent years, firms have made substantial efforts to establish initiatives and mechanism that are aimed at identifying startups' ideas and transferring them into the firms' NPD (Weiblen & Chesbrough, 2015). However, recent research investigating how buying firms can leverage the innovative potential of new ventures points out that creating business relations and conducting projects with startups is anything but a sure-fire success (Zaremba et al., 2017). Originating from the liability of newness, startups possess less routines in interacting with firms and less management skills (Singh et al., 1986). This is accompanied by less manufacturing capabilities and a lack of productive routines to transform their ideas and technologies into reliable products (Terjesen et al., 2011). These liabilities of newness mean that there is a considerable amount of uncertainty for the buying firm in terms of strategic intent, capabilities, as well as product quality when deciding to enter into development partnerships regarding an idea with startups (Zaremba et al., 2017). In contrast, established suppliers can usually draw on a long-lasting business relationship with the respective buying firm, which in turn includes the establishment industry-specific know-how (Gassmann et al., 2010). Given their experience and know-how, fulfilling quality requirements and providing evidence for the technical feasibility of their ideas is usually not an issue (Primo & Amundson, 2002; Ragatz et al., 1997). Furthermore, established suppliers can benefit from accumulated experiences (i.e., learning curve effects) and economies of scale (Zaremba et al., 2016), thus making their ideas and technologies more feasible from the economic standpoint. Whereas ideas generated by suppliers can be described as "close in contextual knowledge distance to the [buying] firm" (Un

& Asakawa, 2015, p. 143) fitting in better with existing technologies and hence might be easier to transfer into NPD while meeting technical and economic requirements (Gassmann et al., 2010; Un et al., 2010), implementing startup ideas is likely to be associated with higher efforts and resources required (if not will lead to cannibalization of existing technologies). A firm has to take these aspects into account when it is faced with the decision which ideas are going to be implemented. Based on these arguments, we predict that:

Hypothesis 3:   *Ideas generated by startups are less likely to be implemented than ideas generated by suppliers.*

2.3. Methodology

2.3.1. Research setting

More than almost any other sector, the automotive industry is recognized for its dependence on suppliers as sources of innovation (Cabigiosu et al., 2013; Yeniyurt et al., 2014). Besides, startups have become increasingly more important for automotive firms helping them to find innovative solutions beyond their established supply base (Homfeldt et al., 2017; Weiblen & Chesbrough, 2015). The automotive manufacturer AUDI AG cooperated in our study and was identified to offer satisfying conditions in order to address our research question properly.

First, the aim to be at the leading edge of automotive innovation and to offer customer appealing products is of high strategic importance and part of the Audi brand strategy (Audi Annual Report, 2015). Second, a central part of the firm's innovation activities concerns the use of both suppliers and startups as external sources of ideas. Moreover, they are strategic partners as the board member for procurement highlights: "We aim to be our suppliers' preferred customer so they come to us first with their innovative ideas […] [and] [w]e share knowledge on technical concepts with our partners right from the pre-development phase" (Audi Annual Report, 2015, p. 72). In addition to established suppliers, the need for non-established, young startup companies as sources of ideas has been recognized and pursued extensively over recent years. Finally, supplier and startup ideas are brought into new products in a systematic manner. New vehicle projects are developed based on a stage-gate model with a robust idea-to-launch process (R. G. Cooper, 2008). A particular focus is on the front end of the innovation process and includes the implementation of open innovation initiatives following a proven, well-established identification and evaluation process. Such initiatives are guided by the innovation management departments of the R&D and purchasing divisions and jointly executed with subject-specific company experts.

While Audi collaborated and enabled access to its innovation management, we were not able to use a controlled experimental design. Rather, the firm agreed to serve as an environment for our study where two of the researchers were given the opportunity to accompany the execution of an open innovation initiative that the firm has initiated. The general procedure of the initiative under study is shown in Figure 3. In addition, we were given access to company records and to the company's idea database that provided an extensive documentation of all supplier and startup ideas with rich information available to test our hypotheses. This naturalistic setting, which is similar to existing studies exploring the quality of innovation ideas (e.g., Björk & Magnusson, 2009; Lilien et al., 2002), thus allowed us to draw on unique data and investigate our research question under real-word conditions.

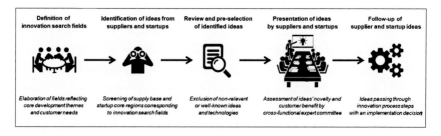

Figure 3: Procedure of the open innovation initiative under study

2.3.2. Data

As noted already, the data for our study refer to an open innovation initiative that was initiated in 2015 and guided by the firm's two innovation management departments. In order to enhance the innovation portfolio for the forthcoming vehicle generation, the decision was made to screen the existing supply base and several startup core regions for innovative ideas based on relevant innovation search fields. Cross-functional workshops with R&D, purchasing, and marketing conducted by the firm led to the definition of several search fields that reflected core development themes and end customer needs. Accordingly, ideas were sought in the fields of "alternative drivetrains and e-mobility", "artificial intelligence and digitalization", "new materials and sustainability", "sensor and safety technologies", as well as "visualization and interaction technologies".

Suppliers from the existing supply base and non-established startup companies from four representative startup regions (China, Israel, Japan/South Korea, United States) were invited to submit and present their ideas, that are, technological solution proposals offered by the external partner for potential further development. Suppliers were addressed by the automotive manufacturer. All relevant supplier firms with development activities fitting the respective search fields were contacted and informed about the initiative. The supplier sample comprised 122 firms worldwide with a wide range of commodity groups given the diversity of innovation search fields. Because suppliers commonly maintain business relations with multiple manufacturers, we are confident that our sample is generally representative for the supplier population. Startups were approached with the help of external scouting partners, such as venture scouting firms and chambers of foreign trade, possessing the required access to startup companies. For each of the four startup regions, an external scouting partner with profound expertise and an extensive network to startups in the respective market was used to identify and contact relevant firms according to the defined innovation search fields (cf. Monteiro & Birkinshaw, 2017). To facilitate idea submission, several information such as descriptions of the innovation search fields were provided as well as a template with which the ideas and technologies were able to be described in basics and re-submitted to the automotive manufacturer. All ideas were then reviewed for their relevance and the firms of the relevant ideas were invited by the automotive manufacturer to personally present their solutions in detail. The process also included the conclusion of non-disclosure agreements if desired in order to protect the knowledge of the idea providers. Given that promising ideas are pursued in the form of joint development projects and potential purchasing contracts, the initiative offered the opportunity to enhance or establish business relations with the automotive manufacturer— incentives that were communicated both to suppliers and startups.

The overall identification process yielded 993 ideas, including 515 ideas from the established supplier sector and 478 ideas from the non-established new venture sector. The 515 supplier ideas were provided by 86 firms, which corresponds to a response rate of 70.5%. In addition, all suppliers that were selected to present their ideas in detail accepted the invitation. The 478 new venture ideas are spread over 472 firms. As the identification of startups was administered by external scouting partners, we cannot determine an accurate "first-contact" response rate. However, from the 149 new venture firms that were invited by the automotive manufacturer to present their ideas, 127 firms participated and thus were willing to share technological details and showed interest to enter into a potential development collaboration.

This represents a response rate of 85.2%. Overall, we can expect that non-response bias is not a concern in our study given such high response rates (Armstrong & Overton, 1977).

As mentioned above, all identified ideas were reviewed for their relevance before entering into the manufacturer's idea evaluation process. Workshop sessions with knowledgeable experts from R&D, purchasing, and marketing were used to review the re-submitted information and to exclude those ideas from the further process that (1) did not fit the respective innovation search fields or (2) were already well-known within the firm. Even though many ideas did not survive this stage, the pre-selection was necessary for several reasons to present unbiased results. For instance, it is not unlikely that also ideas are provided that do not necessarily fit the articulated needs taking the incentive of advancing business relations with a large and reputed manufacturer into account. Further, because there is regular contact between the automotive manufacturer and particularly its established core suppliers, even ideas that were evaluated and decided in the course of previous initiatives might be re-presented. Excluding such ideas was therefore necessary to ensure the comparability of supplier and startup ideas and to avoid any bias in the later assessment. As a result, 350 ideas (199 ideas from 61 suppliers and 151 from 149 new ventures) were selected as being relevant and of potential interest for implementation. Firms of all relevant ideas were invited to personally present their solutions in detail to the automotive manufacturer. For 24 ideas, the respective firms did not follow the invitation, leading to 326 ideas (197 ideas from 61 suppliers1 and 129 ideas from 127 new ventures) that passed through the evaluation process.

Since there is no strict threshold at Audi and in order to consistent with the literature, we reviewed all new ventures regarding their company age to ensure that the term "startup" really applies. As a consequence, we excluded 12 ideas from our analyses provided by firms not meeting the age criterion of maximum eight years (McDougall et al., 1994; Zahra, 1996). Hence, the dataset to test our hypotheses consists of 314 ideas (197 ideas from 61 suppliers[1] and 117 ideas from 115 startups).[2] The average age of the startups in our sample was 3.18 years (std. dev. = 1.84 years), whereas the supplier firms have usually been in existence for several decades (mean = 75.13 years; std. dev. = 61.01 years). The number of employees for more than one-third of startups (40.0%) was between 1 and 10 and for more than another third (36.5%) between 11 and 50. Only five startups (4.3%) had more than 100 employees. In contrast, only

---

[1] This count refers to parent companies and does not consider potential independently operating and innovating subsidiary firms or business units of the respective supplier.

[2] As a robustness check, we reran our models presented in Table 2 and Table 4 with the complete dataset and obtained similar results.

four supplier firms (6.6%) employed fewer than 1,000 people and about one-fourth (26.2%) of the firms had 100,000 employees or more, all of them exceeding $US 10,000 million of annual revenue.[3] This illustrates the differences between the two groups in terms of experience and available resources for idea generation, which is in line with our theoretical underpinning.

2.3.3. Measurement

Dependent variables: novelty, customer benefit, and implementation

In order to allow an adequate idea evaluation, suppliers and startups presented their ideas to cross-functional groups of company experts. To enable personal presentations of all ideas while at the same time keeping the workload for the experts to an acceptable level and preventing negative effects such as "evaluation fatigue", the presentations were spread over five multi-day events comprising more than 150 working hours of presentations. Due to organizational reasons, however, there were overall four events where the startup ideas were presented (one event each for all ideas from each of the four considered startup regions) and one event where all supplier ideas were presented. The presentation procedure was identical throughout the events. To ensure consistent framework conditions, presentation guidelines were provided and the time for each idea presentation was limited to in general 20 minutes followed by a questions and answers section of 10 minutes. The experts were also equipped with the submitted descriptions of the ideas. In order to provide a better understanding of their ideas and technologies, suppliers and startups were asked to show prototypes or proof of concept if applicable. Whereas this approach might be subject to a presenter bias, it is likewise questionable whether a paper-based assessment would be appropriate: as one contact person within innovation emphasized that the true value of in part complex technological ideas cannot be assessed only based on a description. In particular presentation formats, also referred to as "pitches", are suitable to gain a more in-depth understanding of the underlying idea and are therefore widely used in innovation practice (Weiblen & Chesbrough, 2015).

Directly after the presentation, each respective idea was evaluated according to the criteria: *novelty* (degree of innovation, i.e., the extent to which the idea/technology is new and different from existing solutions on a scale from "1 – very low" to "5 – very high" novelty) and *customer benefit* (automotive customer impact, i.e., the extent to which the idea/technology

---

[3] Company data for startups are based on information provided by the external scouting partners and were validated with publicly available information. Supplier data are based on publicly available information, such as annual reports. Suppliers' number of employees and revenues refer to fiscal year of initial contact.

creates value to end consumers on a scale from "1 – very low" to "5 – very high" customer benefit). These criteria and the process by which the ideas are evaluated are well-established within the company.

Given the diversity of innovation search fields and ideas to be evaluated as well as the different extent to which the ideas affected vehicle components, the evaluation committee varied in terms of composition and number of experts, but it was at least three and in a very few cases up to eighteen professionals with both a technical background (R&D professionals) and a business background (purchasers or marketers). In this way, it was ensured that the ideas were evaluated by those professionals who were familiar with the domain (innovation search field) in which the idea was generated (Amabile, 1982; Amabile et al., 1996). The experts were all experienced in evaluating ideas from suppliers and startups. Overall, the evaluation procedure was designed to be interactive: the experts assessed the ideas individually, but they also had the opportunity to discuss their (potentially different) opinions and judgments and based on the joint discussion to adapt and refine their assessments (Franke et al., 2014; Poetz & Schreier, 2012). For each idea and each of the two dimensions, the evaluations were aggregated to an average committee rating that we used for the further analysis (Füller, Hutter, Hautz, & Matzler, 2017). We were able to assess interrater reliability based on overall 2,928 individual ratings among both dimensions by using intraclass correlation (ICC) (Shrout & Fleiss, 1979). Because the ideas were evaluated by varying experts and the number of experts ranged from 3 to 18, we calculated ICC(1) coefficients, each representing one amount of experts. The average ICC for novelty was 0.68 (median = 0.71 with ICCs ranging from 0.21 to 0.91) and for customer benefit 0.69 (median = 0.69 with ICCs ranging from 0.35 to 0.91). Given that the ideas covered a wide range of innovation fields and the ideas were assessed by many different experts from different business divisions all representing different points of view, these statistics are satisfactory for a setting like ours (cf. Amabile et al. (1996); see also Woehr, Loignon, Schmidt, Loughry, and Ohland (2015) pointing out that ICC(1) coefficients are generally characterized by lower values and, in contrast to ICC(2) statistics, hardly reach commonly used reliability cut-offs).

Each idea then passed through the next steps of the firm's frontend of the innovation process working as follows. After the presentation, each idea is pursued separately by those departments in whose field of activity the respective idea falls. The follow-up and subsequent implementation decision focuses on the internal fit as well as technical and economic aspects of each respective idea. Here, the firm is generally interested in whole spectrum of ideas ranging from incremental improvements to radically new solutions. Central to the decision process is whether the ideas match with the internal development roadmap and can fulfil technical and economic target parameters. The follow-up includes internal discussions and bilateral discussions with the respective suppliers and startups, including exchange of samples, initial testing, and creation of a business case. Once sufficiently enough information are gathered, a decision of whether and how the respective idea will be implemented is taken (i.e., joint development project, considering for sourcing). Senior managers in the organizational hierarchy are involved in decision-making. As an idea reaches the implementation status, required resources are allocated to the project for further development and vehicle integration. Hence, the variable implementation serves as holistic quality measure making a statement about the quality of an idea in terms of fitting in with the organization and strategic planning, being technically feasible, as well as creating business opportunities for the manufacturer (see also Salter et al., 2015). Details of the follow-up and the decision regarding each idea has been documented in the idea database. It is worth emphasizing that unlike most studies that simply rely on subjective rater assessments of idea feasibility (Magnusson, 2009; Poetz & Schreier, 2012), we take into account whether ideas were actually decided to be implemented or not by an innovating firm (see also Schemmann, Herrmann, Chappin, & Heimeriks, 2016). Consequently, the variable *implementation* is dichotomous: if an idea was decided to be implemented it is coded as 1, otherwise the idea is coded as 0.

Independent variable: external source of idea

The independent variable of this study is the external source of each respective idea, that is, whether the idea originates from a supplier (i.e., a firm from the existing supply base) or from a startup (i.e., a firm eight years old or younger at the time of initial contact/idea presentation without a pre-existing business relationship to the automotive manufacturer). Accordingly, our independent variable is dichotomous with a value of 1 for all ideas provided by startups and a value of 0 for all ideas coming from suppliers.

Control variables

We include several variables in our analyses to control for possible confounding effects due to individual or situational factors given the naturalistic setting. Because ideas from different domains are included in this study, we control for any effects that the *innovation search fields* might have by including dummy variables in our analysis. This effectively controls for all constant and unmeasured differences across the domains that might explain differences in the variables and relationships investigated, such as origin or type of the idea as well as background of the experts evaluating and pursuing the idea. We also control for the *level of maturity* because more mature ideas might give a better impression of being original, having benefit for end consumers, or might be easier for the firm to implement. Based on information provided by the suppliers and startups, we include a dummy variable for the level of maturity with a value of 1 for all ideas that have already reached the initial proof of concept/prototype stage at the time of presentation and a value of 0 if this was not the case. Furthermore, we consider controls relating to the events in which an idea's novelty and customer benefit were assessed. Note that including dummy variables for the different events is inappropriate because the variables would be the equivalent of our independent variable (because suppliers and startups presented their ideas separately from each other within the events), thus leading to multi-collinearity problems.[4] However, perhaps more importantly, we take account of the *timing of presentation* of an idea within each event as it might influence an idea's assessment, e.g., due to possible learning effects. We include dummy variables for different presentation timings (early, mid, and late) each accounting for one-third of ideas within each event. Because novelty and customer benefit of the ideas were evaluated by an expert committee that varied in terms of composition and number, we also control for these factors. In terms of *committee professional background*, both experts with a technical (R&D experts) and a business background (purchasers or marketers) were part of the committee. Existing research (e.g., Schweisfurth, 2017) suggests to use a balanced set of technical and non-technical experts for assessing ideas, e.g., because an overbalance of technical experts possessing high domain knowledge might undervalue more novel ideas (Moreau, Lehmann, & Markman, 2001). Hence, we consider whether an imbalance of evaluators with a technical background and a business background affects the evaluation result. We measure this with a dummy variable that equals 0 if the idea has been evaluated by the same ratio of technical and economic experts and 1 if the ratio was imbalanced. Furthermore, we include the *number of rating experts*, which can be seen as a proxy for an idea's complexity, as a control variable. In the case of implementation as dependent variable, we do not control for the number of experts but for the *number of different departments* that were involved in the follow-up process and decision of implementation of the respective idea. Here, we also include *novelty* and *customer benefit* as control variables since it is likely that these criteria have an impact on the decision of whether an idea is going to be implemented or not. Finally, the *time until decision* (expressed in months from idea presentation) is used to control for any temporal effects in the decision process.

---

[4] A one-way ANOVA test displayed no significant differences among the four startup events with respect to our key dimensions novelty and customer benefit.

2.4. Analysis and results

We used regression analyses to investigate the effects of whether ideas originate from suppliers or startups on the idea quality dimensions (cf. Schweisfurth, 2017). Table 1 shows the descriptive statistics and correlations of our variables. No indications for problematic levels of multi-collinearity could be found: correlations were within acceptable ranges and the variance inflation factors (VIFs) for the variables were all below 3.00.

OLS regression was used to test hypotheses 1 and 2. The results appear in Table 2. Model 1 includes the relevant control variables: dummies for the innovation search fields, level of maturity, dummies for the timing of presentation, committee professional background, and number of rating experts. Model 2 introduces the independent variable to test for the hypothesized effects. In the case of both novelty and customer benefit as dependent variable, Model 2 provides a good fit as indicated by the significant F value and increasing R^2 after including our independent variable. Regarding novelty, the positive and significant estimated coefficient strongly supports Hypothesis 1, predicting that ideas generated by startups are characterized by a higher degree of novelty than ideas generated by suppliers ($b = 0.235$, $p = 0.006$). In terms of customer benefit, the effect is less strong but still supports Hypothesis 2, which proposes that ideas generated by startups are characterized by a higher degree of customer benefit than ideas generated by suppliers ($b = 0.179$, $p = 0.069$).

We reran our model using quantile regression with the same set of variables (see Table 3). So far, we have supposed that any differences in the dependent variables of novelty and customer benefit are equally important. However, in reality a firm looking for ideas might be interested in a more nuanced picture as it pursues different innovation objectives, e.g., developing radical innovation or rather incremental improvements. Using quantile regression, we can investigate this managerially important question. In terms of novelty, we find negative and significant effects for the 5th and 10th percentile ($b_{5\%} = -0.318$, $p < 0.001$; $b_{10\%} = -0.303$, $p = 0.014$), indicating that supplier ideas can be rather classified as incremental compared to startup ideas. Interestingly, the effect turns over in favor of startup ideas and the coefficient increases the more we move closer to the upper tail of the distribution with the highest value for the 95th percentile ($b_{95\%} = 0.560$, $p < 0.001$). This is in line with managers who search for radical ideas. With respect to customer benefit, we can detect a similar pattern in the data with the strongest effect for the 90th percentile ($b_{90\%} = 0.333$, $p = 0.0014$). Overall, the quantile regression provides further support for Hypotheses 1 and 2..

Table 1: Descriptive statistics and correlations

	1	2	3	4	5	6	7	8	9	10	11	12	13	14	15	16	17
1 Novelty																	
2 Customer benefit	0.42***																
3 Implementation	0.15*	0.13*															
4 External source of idea	0.16**	0.14*	-0.10+														
5 Alternative drivetrains and e-mobility	0.00	-0.26***	-0.07	-0.16**													
6 Artificial intelligence and digitalization	-0.16**	0.12*	0.04	0.15**	-0.32***												
7 New materials and sustainability	0.07	-0.12*	0.05	-0.002	-0.28***	-0.28***											
8 Sensor and safety technologies	0.03	0.08	0.05	-0.01	-0.25***	-0.25***	-0.22***										
9 Visualization and interaction technologies	0.09	0.23***	-0.08	0.03	-0.25***	-0.24***	-0.21***	-0.19**									
10 Level of maturity	0.07	0.02	-0.01	0.14*	0.03	0.11+	0.08	-0.16**	-0.09								
11 Timing of presentation: early	0.01	0.12*	0.08	0.03	0.08	0.26***	-0.15**	-0.12*	-0.12*	0.07							
12 Timing of presentation: mid	-0.08	-0.19**	-0.08	-0.02	0.02	-0.03	-0.06	0.16**	-0.08	-0.03	-0.50***						
13 Timing of presentation: late	0.07	0.08	-0.01	-0.01	-0.10+	-0.23***	0.21***	-0.04	0.20***	-0.04	-0.50***	-0.50***					
14 Committee professional background	0.01	-0.01	0.02	-0.11+	0.01	-0.02	0.02	-0.02	-0.01	-0.04	0.01	0.01	-0.03				
15 Number of rating experts	-0.05	0.15**	-0.02	-0.20***	-0.16**	-0.16**	-0.17**	0.07	0.48***	-0.06	0.01	0.05	-0.06	-0.08			
16 Number of different departments	0.20***	0.19***	0.09	-0.10+	0.02	-0.15*	-0.07	0.15**	0.07	-0.12*	-0.12*	0.18**	-0.06	0.01	0.14*		
17 Time to decision (in months)	0.27***	0.19***	0.07	0.21***	0.06	-0.10+	0.06	-0.07	0.06	-0.05	-0.003	-0.03	0.04	-0.02	-0.02	0.12*	
Mean	3.27	3.12	0.10	0.37	0.25	0.24	0.20	0.17	0.16	0.88	0.33	0.33	0.33	0.82	6.87	3.88	2.85
Standard deviation	0.70	0.85	0.30	0.48	0.43	0.43	0.40	0.37	0.36	0.32	0.47	0.47	0.47	0.38	2.76	1.52	2.44

$N = 314$ ideas.

Significance levels: $^+ p < 0.10$; $^* p < 0.05$; $^{**} p < 0.01$; $^{***} p < 0.001$

Table 2: OLS regression results for novelty and customer benefit as dependent variables

| | Novelty | | | | | | Customer benefit | | | | | |
| | Model 1 | | | Model 2 | | | Model 1 | | | Model 2 | | |
	b	S.E.	β	b	S.E.	β	b	S.E.	β	b	S.E.	β
(Constant)	3.571	(0.238)	***	3.363	(0.248)	***	3.397	(0.271)	***	3.238	(0.284)	***
Alternative drivetrains and e-mobility[a]	-0.283	(0.147)	-0.174 +	-0.185	(0.150)	-0.114	-0.768	(0.167)	-0.391 ***	-0.694	(0.172)	-0.353 ***
Artificial intelligence and digitalization[a]	-0.509	(0.153)	-0.309 **	-0.468	(0.152)	-0.284 **	-0.216	(0.174)	-0.109	-0.185	(0.174)	-0.093
New materials and sustainability[a]	-0.189	(0.149)	-0.108	-0.124	(0.149)	-0.070	-0.599	(0.170)	-0.282 ***	-0.550	(0.171)	-0.259 **
Sensor and safety technologies[a]	-0.159	(0.148)	-0.085	-0.113	(0.148)	-0.060	-0.174	(0.169)	-0.077	-0.139	(0.169)	-0.061
Level of maturity	0.186	(0.124)	0.086	0.140	(0.123)	0.064	0.113	(0.141)	0.043	0.078	(0.142)	0.030
Timing of presentation: early[b]	0.071	(0.104)	0.048	0.055	(0.104)	0.037	0.058	(0.119)	0.032	0.045	(0.119)	0.025
Timing of presentation: mid[b]	-0.064	(0.100)	-0.043	-0.077	(0.100)	-0.052	-0.316	(0.114)	-0.176 **	-0.325	(0.114)	-0.182 **
Committee professional background	0.001	(0.102)	0.001	0.037	(0.102)	0.020	0.003	(0.117)	0.001	0.030	(0.117)	0.014
Number of rating experts	-0.032	(0.017)	-0.126 +	-0.019	(0.017)	-0.075	0.014	(0.019)	0.044	0.023	(0.020)	0.076
External source of idea[c]				0.235	(0.086)	0.163 **				0.179	(0.098)	0.102 +
R^2	0.055			0.078			0.163			0.172		
Adjusted R^2	0.027			0.047			0.138			0.145		
F value	1.961	*		2.555	**		6.585	***		6.304	***	

$N = 314$ ideas.

b = unstandardized coefficient, S.E. = standard error, β = standardized coefficient.

[a] With innovation search field "visualization and interaction technologies" as reference category.

[b] With "timing of presentation: late" as reference category.

[c] Coding of independent variable: 0 = idea originates from a supplier; 1 = idea originates from a startup.

Significance levels: + $p < 0.10$; * $p < 0.05$; ** $p < 0.01$; *** $p < 0.001$.

Table 3: Quantile regression results for novelty and customer benefit

	Novelty													
	5%		10%		25%		50%		75%		90%		95%	
	b	S.E.	b	S.E.	b	S.E.	b	S.E.	b	S.E.	b	S.E.	b	S.E.
(Constant)	2.151	(0.693) **	2.684	(0.434) ***	3.048	(0.341) ***	3.377	(0.190) ***	3.560	(0.242) ***	4.115	(0.235) ***	4.347	(0.319) ***
External source of idea[a]	-0.318	(0.091) ***	-0.303	(0.122) *	0.042	(0.149)	0.457	(0.115) ***	0.438	(0.053) ***	0.500	(0.091) ***	0.560	(0.075) ***
Pseudo-R^2 (Koenker and Machado)	0.068		0.089		0.046		0.060		0.118		0.054		0.169	
	Customer benefit													
	5%		10%		25%		50%		75%		90%		95%	
	b	S.E.	b	S.E.	b	S.E.	b	S.E.	b	S.E.	b	S.E.	b	S.E.
(Constant)	1.720	(0.434) ***	2.088	(0.389) ***	2.750	(0.326) ***	3.420	(0.263) ***	3.717	(0.334) ***	4.378	(0.493) ***	5.168	(0.466) ***
External source of idea[a]	-0.108	(0.164)	-0.157	(0.116)	0.014	(0.124)	0.080	(0.133)	0.270	(0.141) +	0.333	(0.103) **	0.271	(0.130) *
Pseudo-R^2 (Koenker and Machado)	0.173		0.171		0.194		0.126		0.076		0.063		0.095	

$N = 314$ ideas.
All models include the same control variables as in the OLS regression (see Table 2).
[a] Coding of independent variable: 0 = idea originates from a supplier; 1 = idea originates from a startup.
Significance levels: + $p < 0.10$; * $p < 0.05$; ** $p < 0.01$; *** $p < 0.001$.

To test hypothesis 3, we conducted binary logistic regression given that the dependent variable under investigation is binary, asking whether an idea was implemented or not. Table 4 reports the estimated effect parameters and results of Wald tests on their significance. Model 1 contains the relevant controls: dummies for the innovation search fields, level of maturity, number of different departments pursuing an idea, novelty, customer benefit, and time to decision. The independent variable is included in model 2 to examine the effect of the idea origin on implementation. Model 2 provides a better fit with the addition of our independent variable as indicated by the declining log-likelihood value as well as the increasing significant chi-square value and increasing Nagelkerke's R^2. In line with existing research (Schemmann et al., 2016), novelty of an idea is positively associated with its chance of being implemented (b = 0.890, odds ratio exp(b) = 2.435, p = 0.025). Most importantly, the negative and significant coefficient of our external source dummy reveals an even more strong effect and supports Hypothesis 3, predicting that ideas generated by startups are less likely to be implemented than ideas generated by suppliers (b = -1.525, odds ratio exp(b) = 0.218, p = 0.006).

Table 4: Binary logistic regression results for implementation as dependent variable

	Implementation					
	Model 1			Model 2		
	b	S.E.		b	S.E.	
(Constant)	-7.092	(1.587)	***	-7.912	(1.703)	***
Alternative drivetrains and e-mobility[a]	1.068	(0.914)		0.831	(0.926)	
Artificial intelligence and digitalization[a]	1.762	(0.858)	*	1.927	(0.871)	*
New materials and sustainability[a]	1.736	(0.877)	*	1.571	(0.889)	+
Sensor and safety technologies[a]	1.565	(0.854)	+	1.637	(0.861)	+
Level of maturity	-0.355	(0.625)		-0.117	(0.638)	
Number of departments	0.139	(0.125)		0.083	(0.125)	
Novelty	0.561	(0.341)	+	0.890	(0.398)	*
Customer benefit	0.394	(0.291)		0.387	(0.303)	
Time to decision (in months)	0.014	(0.071)		0.084	(0.075)	
External source of idea[b]				-1.525	(0.556)	**
Pseudo-R^2 (Nagelkerke)	0.110			0.167		
-2 log likelihood	185.532			176.510		
Chi-square (df)	16.857 (9)		+	25.879 (10)		**

N = 314 ideas.
[a]With innovation search field "visualization and interaction technologies" as reference category.
[b]Coding of independent variable: 0 = idea originates from a supplier; 1 = idea originates from a startup.
Significance levels: $^+ p \leq 0.10$; $* p < 0.05$; $** p < 0.01$; $*** p < 0.001$.

Our results reveal that, even though startup ideas perform better with regard to novelty and customer benefit, the creative performance alone is not enough and there are particularly factors relating to the internal fit and economic performance as well as proof of the technical feasibility of the respective idea that tip the scales for implementation – factors in which startup ideas obviously lose out to supplier ideas. The innovation idea "Holographic Display Technology" offered by a startup and belonging to the search field visualization and interaction technologies is exemplary for this observation. The technology, which was initially developed for mobile devices, enables the projection of holographic imagery coming out of a screen, including touch and interaction functionality with no need for any eye-wear or special gears. The idea was evaluated very high in terms of novelty and customer benefit. Even though there were several use cases fitting the automotive context, the startup idea differed from well-established solutions and could not satisfy the internal automotive quality standards. The adaption of this idea thus would have required a considerable amount of resources with an uncertain outcome of technical feasibility and economic added value. In contrast, the supplier idea "Innovative Lightweight Tire", belonging to the search field new materials and sustainability, was decided for implementation even though evaluated slightly worse in terms of novelty and customer benefit. Beneficially, this supplier idea fitted in with an existing component and improved it in a way that created enhanced business opportunities for the automotive manufacturer. Due to special material use and configuration, the overall weight and material consumption could be reduced while at the same time meeting the determined technical performance and cost parameters. Still, even though the ideas coming from startups were less likely to be implemented than ideas provided by suppliers, the implemented startup ideas scored higher in terms of novelty (mean$_{startups}$ = 4.07 versus mean$_{suppliers}$ = 3.43, t = 2.762, p = 0.010). However, no significant difference with respect to customer benefit was found among the ideas to be implemented (mean$_{startups}$ = 3.71 versus mean$_{suppliers}$ = 3.38, t = 1.285, p = 0.214).

2.5. Conclusion and implications

In recent years, many firms have begun to tap beyond their existing supply base and increasingly draw on the potential of startups as an additional source of ideas to their established suppliers. Motivated by this phenomenon, our study has examined how the ideas generated by both external parties perform compared to each other in terms of key quality dimensions. The relevance of this question is high, because the results provide guidance to decision makers whether or not to go a more uncertain way and invest in the identification of and collaboration with non-established startup companies. Based on a unique real-world empirical comparison of 314 supplier and startup ideas, we have found empirical evidence that ideas generated by startups are characterized by a higher degree of novelty and end customer benefit compared to ideas generated by established suppliers. Findings from quantile regression underline this superiority by showing that startup ideas particularly perform better when focusing on more novel and customer appealing ideas, which is in line with managers looking for radical ideas. On the downside, we find that startup ideas are less likely to be implemented, which implies that supplier ideas provide a better fit with existing technologies and create more valuable business opportunities while meeting technical and economic criteria. However, ideas from startups that were selected for implementation were still more novel. Our study is the first to empirically show these results for a large scale idea dataset, thereby providing valuable theoretical and managerial contributions.

2.5.1. Contributions to theory

Our study contributes to the growing literature on open innovation and external knowledge sourcing in three important ways. First, we add to the emerging stream of research on the use of startups as external sources of ideas by showing how their ideas differ from those ideas provided by established peers in a specific open innovation context. Existing research has only recently started to investigate how startups and their technological ideas can be identified (Monteiro & Birkinshaw, 2017; Weiblen & Chesbrough, 2015) as well as how firms can leverage the potential of innovative startups and integrate them into their existing supply base (Zaremba et al., 2017). Our study adds the puzzle piece of how startups perform and thus responds to the call for research on startups' innovative capabilities in the early stages of a firm's innovation process (Kickul et al., 2011). Taking established suppliers as opponents, we show that startups indeed constitute promising open innovation partners that can deliver novel and customer appealing ideas for certain innovation fields in which a firm aims to innovate. Accordingly, we also add to the research on local versus distant search (Katila & Ahuja, 2002) and provide evidence that drawing on knowledge from more distant domains, that is, from beyond the established supply base, facilitates the identification of promising solutions.

Second, we contribute to theory by examining the involvement of suppliers in the front end of the NPD process, an area that has remained largely unexplored. Although this phase, in which new product ideas are identified and generated, has been recognized as crucial to the success of innovation projects (van den Ende, Frederiksen, & Prencipe, 2015; Verworn, 2009), only less attention has been paid to the involvement of suppliers in this NPD stage. According to Wowak et al. (2016, p. 67), neglecting the role of suppliers in the early stages of NPD "has created a gap in scholarly understanding". While there is extensive research that considers the supplier as a co-development partner (Koufteros et al., 2005; Lau et al., 2010) providing input in various NPD stages (Al-Zu'bi & Tsinopoulos, 2012), studies on the specific involvement and subsequent outcome of suppliers in the front end of the NPD process as a source of ideas have just started to appear (Homfeldt et al., 2017; Schoenherr & Wagner, 2016; Wagner, 2012). We add to this evolving discipline by examining supplier contributions in the early stages and thus provide a better understanding of the value of ideas generated by suppliers.

Third, taking the two accounts above in tandem, we contribute to the creation of a more holistic view on the value of the diverse set of external sources of ideas. While the existing innovation literature concentrates solely on comparing the quality of ideas generated by different user types (Lilien et al., 2002; Magnusson, 2009; Poetz & Schreier, 2012; Schweisfurth, 2017), our study is the first to consider suppliers and startups as increasingly important external sources of ideas. We believe this is an important contribution to the field of open innovation where past research and future directions are highly focused on users as open innovation partners [see also the recent literature reviews of Bogers et al. (2017) and Randhawa et al. (2016)].

2.5.2. Implications for managerial practice

Our study has implications for managers who are developing strategies that aim at accessing and exploiting innovation ideas from external partners. The findings suggest that firms in need of ideas for new products are recommended to reach beyond their established supply base and integrate startups in the ideation phase of their innovation process. While such an approach can facilitate the identification of exceptionally novel and customer appealing ideas, the beneficial outcomes might occur at the expense of realization. Although we did not provide a detailed analysis of reasons for what makes the implementation so difficult, firms must be prepared that bringing startup ideas into the final product is a challenging and resource-intensive undertaking. If firms want to gain a competitive advantage through startup integration, they must be willing to invest resources in the implementation of startup ideas and ensure to have the required mechanisms and mind-sets that enable the transfer and handling of knowledge from beyond the established supply base. To enhance the chance of implementing startup ideas, a useful approach for a firm can also be to encourage collaborations between its established suppliers and promising startups, thus combining the specific strengths of both parties and boosting new venture performance as it is shown by Song and Di Benedetto (2008). This approach becomes even more relevant if a startup idea is not directly exploitable or adaptable by the buying firm. In that case, handing over the development responsibility (including the achievement of technical and economic target parameters) to an established supplier would save opportunities for the buying firm to profit from startup innovation.

While our results justify the integration of startups in the ideation phase, it is not to say that they can or should replace established suppliers. The firm's innovation strategy must depend on its objectives. When the goal is radical innovation, startups unequivocally constitute a promising source. However, in many cases incremental improvements to existing solutions, which are more likely to come from suppliers, are often not too costly and therefore considered to be quick wins by the organization. From an overall perspective, we therefore suggest that the ideal approach for a successful firm innovation portfolio is the use of both partner types.

2.6. Limitations and future research

Despite its theoretical and managerial contributions, our study is not without limitations, which in turn provide potential avenues for future research. First, our sample is comprised of ideas identified, evaluated, and pursued in the course of an open innovation initiative conducted in a single automotive firm. Although we consider Audi and the setting as quite representative for other large firms and initiatives (ideation was based on diverse innovation search fields in a complex industry), we are aware that the generalizability of our results is limited. More empirical research in different firms and industries is hence needed to validate our findings. In particular, studies in different (less mature) industrial contexts (e.g., consumer goods sector) would deepen our understanding whether the capability of startups and suppliers to provide promising ideas is influenced by the underlying product category or industry sector.

Second, a trade-off in our study is the naturalistic setting that strengthens external validity at the cost of internal validity. Although we controlled for possible confounding factors, future work may use controlled experimental designs for further confirmation and elaboration of our results. For instance, whereas the evaluations in our study are in great-parts based on the impressions gained during the personal presentations of suppliers and startups, experimental studies usually rely on paper-based assessments where experts evaluate each idea blind to the source. However, we believe that in a setting like ours, where highly technology-driven ideas had to be assessed, an evaluation only based on an idea description would not be appropriate. In addition, it would be interesting to see what exactly motivates startups and suppliers to participate in the early stages of a firm's NPD process and to provide ideas of high quality (LaBahn & Krapfel, 2000). While in our setting suppliers and startups were equally motivated by the fact to advance business relations, future research might control different motivational factors, whether it is incentives or rather relational aspects. Furthermore, future studies may also consider the internal ideators at a company to provide a more comprehensive view of closed versus open innovation outcomes in ideation (Schweisfurth, 2017).

Third, while we were able to provide a better understanding of the value of ideas generated by suppliers compared to ideas generated by startups in terms of key quality dimensions, our study is limited in figuring out the impact of involving both partners and using their ideas on the success of a firm's final output, that are, the technologies and products introduced into the market. Future studies might use survey formats to investigate the comparative effect of startup and supplier involvement on a firm's financial performance or other performance measures (see, e.g., Al-Zu'bi and Tsinopoulos (2012) who examine the relative impact of integrating suppliers and lead users in the NPD process on a firm's product variety).

Finally, our results indicate obstacles with regard to the implementation of startup ideas but without providing a detailed analysis of reasons in the specific context (e.g., technical, economic, relational, lack of know-how). Hence, qualitative longitudinal studies covering the process from idea generation to implementation should be used to better understand why an implementation fails or how an implementation works successfully, thus providing helpful guidance to practitioners.

Chapter 3 – Identifying partners outside existing networks: How do corporate organizations search for startups?

Abstract:

The search for external knowledge has evolved to a strategic task for corporations. Startups are a source for particularly novel knowledge and product ideas. Our article analyzes how corporations search for startups. We conduct a multiple case study among eight firms within the automotive industry. Results highlight (1) four organizational approaches, (2) a detailed identification process, and (3) various search instruments to identify startups. We differentiate into four push and seven pull instruments, such as the organization of startup pitch events or the establishment of networks to relevant partners. Our findings add to the literature on external knowledge sourcing by highlighting how organizations search for knowledge outside their networks. As we show three internal approaches to organize the search for startups, we expand boundary spanning literature, which has primarily focused on external scouting units embedded in local startup environments.

3.1. Introduction

External sources of knowledge have become a necessary extension to internal innovation activities (Monteiro et al., 2017; Rosenkopf & Nerkar, 2001). Collaborations with customers, suppliers, universities, or even competitors are a promising way to extend the own knowledge base in order to increase the firm's innovativeness (Felin & Zenger, 2014; Laursen & Salter, 2006). Recently, startups as a specific knowledge provider have received growing attention (Weiblen & Chesbrough, 2015; Zaremba et al., 2016). By collaborating with startups, corporations hope to benefit from the startups' entrepreneurial characteristics, such as alertness, creativity, flexibility, and willingness to take risks (Audretsch et al., 2014; Criscuolo et al., 2012; Marion et al., 2012).

Firms looking for innovative ideas search within distinct search spaces, which differ according to their proximity of existing knowledge (Knudsen & Srikanth, 2014). Local search builds on knowledge already in use (Stuart & Podolny, 1996), while distant search expands existing knowledge and often builds on external stimuli (Fleming & Sorenson, 2004; Rosenkopf & Nerkar, 2001). The literature on search for external knowledge analyzes the impact of various knowledge providers on firms' innovation performance (Laursen & Salter, 2006; Leiponen & Helfat, 2010). In addition, prior studies have also shown that knowledge provided by startups increases the innovation performance of corporations (Dushnitsky & Lenox, 2006; Wadhwa et al., 2016). Apart from these outcome-based investigations, scholars have also focused on how corporate firms identify innovative partners within their networks (Pulles et al., 2014; Schiele, 2006). Still, we lack understanding on how firms search for new innovation partners outside their networks such as startups. Some research has focused on the identification of startups, but is limited to mechanisms within external organizational structures such as external scouting or sensing units (Gassmann & Gaso, 2004; Monteiro & Birkinshaw, 2017). As no prior study provides a holistic picture of approaches to identify startups, our research addresses the following main question: *How do corporations search for startups?*

To answer the research question, we conduct a multiple-case study among 8 automotive multinational corporations in Germany. Results show external and internal organizational structures that are established within corporations and various instruments to identify startups, such as pitch events and networks. By focusing on startups as a single source of external knowledge, we contribute to recent calls to better understand the activities necessary to search for innovative partners (Monteiro & Birkinshaw, 2017). Thus, we expand our knowledge mainly limited to the outcome of search activities. Further, we extend boundary spanning literature by showing three internal approaches to embed scouting units in order to initiate knowledge flow to the organization. From a managerial perspective, our results display how corporations identify startups in order to maintain their firm's position in dynamic market situations (Anderson & Tushman, 1990; Bergek et al., 2013).

The paper is structured in the following way. First, we analyze literature on external knowledge sourcing in the context of corporate-startup relationships as well as boundary spanning literature. The following part describes the framing of the study and data. Next, we show the results of the study by illustrating organizational approaches, a search process and search instruments. The paper ends with a discussion of implications and future research directions.

3.2. Theoretical background

3.2.1. External knowledge sourcing and the search for startups

Accessing external knowledge has evolved to an essential part of firms' overall strategies (Basu, Phelps, & Kotha, 2016; van Wijk et al., 2008). Various empirical studies show the positive impact of external knowledge on the innovation performance of the sourcing firm (Ahuja & Katila, 2001; Laursen & Salter, 2006, 2014). Corporate-startup collaborations differ in their closeness, flexibility and equity-involvement which has implications on their reversibility as well as the necessary commitment (Van de Vrande, Lemmens, & Vanhaverbeke, 2006; Van de Vrande, Vanhaverbeke, & Duysters, 2009). Prior research describes strategic alliances (Lavie, 2007; Stuart, 2000), CVC investments (Dushnitsky & Lenox, 2006; Wadhwa & Basu, 2013) and acquisitions (Andersson & Xiao, 2016) as successful ways to access external knowledge. But knowledge from distant industries and unknown partners such as startups becomes more important (Brunswicker & Hutschek, 2010; Gassmann et al., 2010). Therefore, corporations have started to create specific program-based collaborations, such as accelerators and incubators, to access startups' knowledge (Bergek & Norrman, 2008; Pauwels et al., 2016).

But why are startups a valuable source of external knowledge? Due to missing assets, experimentation with a large number of ideas is not possible (Marion et al., 2012; van Burg et al., 2012). Hence, startups are enforce to conduct focused and dynamic new product development (A. C. Cooper, 1981; Freeman & Engel, 2007; Rothaermel, 2002). Newly developed products increase startups' legitimacy, allow to quickly access market shares and generate early cash flows to sustain survival (Schoonhoven et al., 1990). Thus, innovation capability is a critical variable for startup performance (Chrisman et al., 1998). Further, startups' flexibility is ensured by its organizational structure, including short chains of command, due to its small firm's size (Kickul et al., 2011; Rothaermel, 2002). As startups possess willingness to take risks and high growth potential, they accomplish a prime position for innovation, especially disruptive innovation (Criscuolo et al., 2012; Engel, 2011). Thus, forming ties and acquiring knowledge of startups "can be an important source for innovation and growth for the established firm" (Weiblen & Chesbrough, 2015, p. 88).

In order to access this important source of innovation and growth, corporations have installed processes and apply search instruments (Homfeldt et al., 2017; Rohrbeck, Hölzle, & Gemünden, 2009). Scouting for external technologies and startups is conducted in an early phase of innovation processes and consists of identification, selection and evaluation (Rohrbeck et al., 2009; Salerno, de Vasconcelos Gomes, da Silva, Bagno, & Freitas, 2015). Lichtenthaler (2005) describes a six step search process to identify diversification opportunities, divided into: (1) definitions of search fields, (2) identification of business ideas, (3) validation of business ideas, (4) rough assessment of business ideas, (5) detailed analysis of business ideas, and (6) decision making. Some instruments to identify startups are described in literature, e.g., AT&T Foundry identifies interesting startups "through the Foundry's network or through a response to a call for proposals in a certain problem area" (Weiblen & Chesbrough, 2015, p. 73). Further, the role of (technology) scouts (Pauwels et al., 2016; Rohrbeck, 2010), scouting-units (Monteiro & Birkinshaw, 2017) and startup pitch events (Homfeldt et al., 2017; Weiblen & Chesbrough, 2015) have received attention in prior research.

3.2.2. Boundary spanning to transfer knowledge of startups

Boundary spanning on an organizational level describes the openness of organizations towards external sources of knowledge (Dollinger, 1984; Leifer & Delbecq, 1978). Through boundary spanning, firms can access knowledge or capabilities to face current and future market needs (Rosenkopf & Nerkar, 2001). Prior research addresses the question on how individuals collect and channel external knowledge to make it accessible for internal units (Tushman, 1977; Tushman & Scanlan, 1981). Another research stream analyzes the inter- and intra-firm interaction of teams (Ancona & Caldwell, 1988, 1992). On the one hand, boundary spanners, such as individuals, departments, or business units, can be allocated close to current business practice, which ensures a good link to internal experts (Hill & Birkinshaw, 2014). On the other hand, boundary spanners may be located outside the organization, e.g., within a specific business unit or a scouting satellite, so that they are close to external sources of knowledge (Basu et al., 2016; Keil, Maula, Schildt, & Zahra, 2008). For our study we define boundary spanning unit as a "specialized entity that mediates the flow of information between relevant actors in the focal organization and the task environment" (Monteiro & Birkinshaw, 2017, p. 344).

3.3. Method

The purpose of our research is to provide a holistic picture on how to identify startups as innovation partners by describing the underlying organizational structures and implementation of search. We conducted a multiple case study mainly based on interviews with experts within the field of startup management from the corporation's perspective (Eisenhardt, 1989; Yin, 2014).

3.3.1. Design and sample

Our sample consists of major firms within the German automotive industry. The automotive industry is recognized as one of the fastest changing and most innovative industries in the world, with corporations spending huge amounts of resources on the identification and development of innovations (Hüttinger et al., 2014; Ili, Albers, & Miller, 2010). To establish a certain degree of variation and maintain comparability in our sample, we applied a theoretical sampling approach (Patton, 2002). We considered two original equipment manufacturers (OEMs) as well as six major first-tier supplier, which are listed among the 100 biggest automotive suppliers globally. Hence, we followed the assumption that larger corporations are the first to develop approaches to search for startups due to resource availability and needs for external knowledge. For an overview of the sample see Table 5.

3.3.2. Data collection

Data were collected in two phases. In the first phase, based on secondary data, insights on the selected cases were obtained, which served as case-specific preparation for the interviews (Eisenhardt & Graebner, 2007; Yin, 2014). Secondary data consist of publicly available materials, e.g., articles, Crunchbase, CB Insights and company websites. These data allowed us to illustrate the corporations' fields of interest and possible collaboration approaches. In the second phase, 13 in-depth semi-structured interviews were conducted. We followed a key informant approach including employees from innovation management, R&D, procurement,

M&A, strategy, and CVC units (John & Reve, 1982). A structured interview guideline was used (see 9.1. Appendix Chapter 3). Two researchers participated in the interviews, which were then recorded and transcribed. In total, the interviews yielded 10 hours of voice recording and 196 pages of transcript.

Table 5: Sample

Firm*	Product portfolio	Revenues (2016; B €)	Job title of interview partners	Duration of interviews
A	Supplier exterior components	10-50	(1) Head of strategy	52 min.
B	Supplier electronics & software	> 50	(1) Investment partner (2) Procurement manager	68 min. 50 min.
C	Supplier exterior components	10-50	(1) Senior manager M&A (2) Manager corporate strategy	51 min. 45 min.
D	Supplier powertrain components	10-50	(1) R&D manager (2) Head of corporate strategy	43 min. 43 min.
E	Supplier exterior & interior components	<10	(1) R&D manager	52 min.
F	Supplier electronics	<10	(1) R&D manager	48 min.
G	Car manufacturer	10-50	(1) Procurement manager (2) Director partnering	24 min. 44 min.
H	Car manufacturer	> 50	(1) Manager business innovation (2) Manager technology scouting	52 min. 22 min.

*all firms are headquartered in Germany and belong to the automotive industry

3.3.3. Data analysis

One of the authors coded all interviews before discussing the codes with the co-authors. First, each case was analyzed individually to make sense of the data by structuring, defining, and reducing the collected information. In the following, the corporations' organizational structure, processes, and instruments to identify startups were defined. After the single case analysis, the cross-case comparison followed. Therefore, we continuously reviewed all interview transcripts. Based on the detected similarities and differences qualitative statements on corporations' search approaches were abstracted. To ensure reliability, we discussed the deducted codes with industry experts, entrepreneurs, and academic scholars (Eisenhardt, 1989).

3.4. Results

Our results highlight (1) four different organizational structures, (2) one search process, and (3) various instruments used to identify innovative startups. We thereby address relevant topics as the investment manager of Corporation B put it: *"(we need) more systematization, let's say, more standardization with appropriate tool support. "*

3.4.1. Organizational approaches

Corporations use various organizational structures to identify startups. We identify four distinct approaches which can be independent organizational entities (referred to as central unit) or part of existing units (decentralized unit). Decentralized approaches can imply single or multiple business units, such as R&D, procurement, M&A, or corporate strategy. Table 6 provides an overview of the four organizational approaches.

Table 6: Organizational approaches

Structure	Description	Coupling to internal customers	Flexibility and speed
Decentralized – single functional	• Experts from one single department (such as R&D, procurement, or M&A) involved • Less systematic and standardized processes	Strong	Low
Decentralized – cross-functional	• Involvement of cross-departmental teams (including, e.g., R&D, procurement, M&A, and corporate strategy) • Systematic development of search field and approach based on internal demands and trends	Strong	Low
Central – internal	• Definition of search fields and monitoring of startup environment centrally • Extensive communication among departments	Moderate	Moderate
Central – external	• Establishment of an external unit, such as a CVC unit, scouting satellite, or listening post • Extensive communication between internal and external department	Weak	High

Most of the time, setting up decentralized structures are initial steps to start searching for startups. As the expert of Corporation F: *"(The corporation) decided to integrate technology and innovation management within our R&D department. Therefore, there is no central innovation management [...] there is no separate function for technology scouting or startup monitoring. "* In contrast, centrally managed units pool demands and support trend scouting. Central units can be organized internally as own entities, which follow exclusively innovation tasks, such as technology and startup scouting. In addition to internal units, CVC or listening units exist and are examples for external units as they are located outside the organizational boundaries of a firm. An investment partner at Corporation B describes the role of such a unit in the following way: *"[...] everything concerning startups runs through this department [...]*

(and we) get in direct contact with startups." However, this organizational structure requires a strong link to internal stakeholders. We highlight specific differences regarding the flexibility and speed of these approaches. Further, we distinguish the coupling to internal customers, e.g., R&D or M&A experts, who are responsible for investments or partnering with startups.

3.4.2. Identification process

Our study shows that corporations have established distinct processes to operationalize their search for startups. The various search processes are resembling and consist of the three main steps: definition of search fields, systematic search for startups, and evaluation. Search processes for startups start with internal demands or external opportunities such as described by the interviewed procurement manager of Corporation B: "*[...] technical departments, have some technical questions, problems. We then search for external knowledge providers. (Further we) derived (search fields) from mega-trends [...].*" Internal demands result in search fields focusing on specific problems. By being less specific, firms allow broader search and enhance their chance to identify more distant knowledge (Criscuolo et al., 2017). Depending on their resources, corporations pick search instruments and decide how broad and intensive their search is designed. After applying these instruments, corporations end up with various ideas provided by different startups. These ideas are then validated and pre-selected accordingly: "*[...] the first pre-filter is of course, does it (the startup innovation) fit to our search fields.*" (Corporation D, interviewee 2) Finally, depending on the type of collaboration, a thorough evaluation is conducted. Building on the identified approaches, we offer a consolidated identification process consisting of seven steps as illustrated in Figure 4.

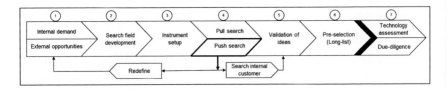

Figure 4: Identification process

3.4.3. Search instruments

Our analysis of established search instruments focuses on the design, effort, and output, as well as benefits and problems. By distinguishing in "pull" and "push instruments", we follow recent terminology for instruments within open innovation (Homfeldt et al., 2017; Wagner & Bode, 2014). While pull instruments require the initiative of corporations and active search, push instruments are rather passive, e.g., in a way that startups are introduced by external partners. The following section describes the identified instruments in detail (see Table 7 for an overview).

The first identified pull instrument is desk research. Most corporations start to search for startups by *"continuous screening of web-based sources"* (Corporation G, interviewee 1). An investment partner at Corporation B describes that they *"currently try to professionalize (startup scouting) by a web-crawler, which is able to scan for various search criteria within various media, especially within the internet."* Web-crawlers imply higher cost compared to simple web-searches. Still, the yield of the instrument is a continuous screening of market deal-flows, limited to previously defined keywords. In order to enrich web-based search results, corporations buy external startup database services.

Moreover, corporation uses *"scientific publications [...] to spot interesting startups"* (interviewee of Corporation E). Experts within corporations visit scientific conferences to spot new technologies, talent and spin-offs. This instrument allows to spot future technology developments in an early stage. Similar are visits of trade fairs and exhibitions. These instruments requires an internal employee to visit startup fairs, conferences, and open pitch events. Often, these kind of events are organized by external service providers in order to connect startups to potential industry partners and investors. Without preparation, the outcome of visiting fairs and conferences is rather limited. However, by *"using a process, following the event catalog, [...] dividing responsibilities across participants, [...] and drawing up a summary of the event"* (Corporation D, interviewee 1), startup events are a good opportunity to set up first contacts. Furthermore, these events are an opportunity to build network connections and communicate the corporation's interest in collaborating with startups as new business partners.

Another pull instrument are self-organized pitch events. Depending on the setting of this instrument, startups and internal experts of the corporation get in first contact and have the opportunity to discuss, for example, the commercial and technical aspects of the startups' innovation. As the pitching startups are often pre-selected, the quality of startups and their fit to the searching organization are usually very high.

In addition, our results show that corporations invest in funds, referred to as fund of funds, to continuously screen market deal-flow. The application of this instrument is described by an investment partner of Corporation B: *"We invested [...] to benefit from their expertise and screen their deal-flow, this gives us the opportunity to match (startups to our search fields)."* Corporations also invest in the service of external scouting partners. These partners search for startups *"based on previously developed scouting request"* (Corporation C, interviewee 1). Requests are mostly based on corporations' search fields and startups are matched by external scouting partners. External scouting services are assumed to be highly professional, yielding in high search outcome.

The last pull-instrument are scouting satellites, which are external units set up within startup "hot-spots", like the Silicon Valley or Israel. These units are set up to establish close links to the relevant startup environment and allows the corporations to build close collaborations with relevant players (Monteiro & Birkinshaw, 2017).

We also identified four push instruments. The first is networking with business partners as an instrument to identify innovative startups. In this case, potentially interesting startups are communicated, e.g., through partner within the supply chain. The R&D manager of Corporation D describes that they have a *"network with original equipment manufacturers and suppliers, exchanging information concerning a specific field of interest, where we just receive a phone call, asking for corporations' interest into a specific startup."* Thereby, corporations are able to identify startups with minor efforts. However, they are dependent on the professional startup management skills of their suppliers. Other partners are venture capitalists. Furthermore, corporations use networks with non-partnering firms in order to identify innovative start-ups. This instrument describes the practice to build networks with customers, competitors, or corporations form other industries, which communicate information about relevant startups. In addition, organizations use networks to universities, public, or non-profit research institutes to identify emerging startups, especially using *"direct contacts to university professors"* (interviewee of Corporation E).

Another passively managed push instrument to identify startups are landing- or web-pages. Thereby, corporations are contacted by startups that are searching for new business partners. The establishment of such a contact possibility requires low effort by the corporation: *"on the webpage the startup is asked to provide general information [...] (which are) automatically transferred into a database"* (Corporation H, interviewee 1). However, there is no opportunity for the corporation to filter the received applications, leading to a high effort in selecting the detected startups afterwards.

Table 7: Search instruments

Instrument	Description	Continuous deal-flow	Effort	Output	Benefits	Drawbacks
Pull instruments						
Desk research	Manual web-based search, automatic web screening, and external database services	Y	Low	Low	▪ Continuous screening of market deal-flow ▪ Little implementation costs	▪ Depends on quality and breadth of database ▪ Time consuming
Scientific conferences/ publications	Visits of scientific conferences, reviewing publications	Y	Moderate	Moderate	▪ Identification of startups in an early stage ▪ Access to distant knowledge (different industries)	▪ Requires profound knowledge ▪ Time consuming
Trade fairs/ exhibitions	Visits of trade fairs and exhibitions	N	Moderate	Moderate	▪ Fast screening of many startups ▪ Complementary marketing effect	▪ Preparation and post processing efforts ▪ Time consuming
Self-organized pitch events	Organizing startup events with open registration or professional search and pre-selection	N	High	Moderate	▪ Direct exchange between internal experts and startups ▪ Intensive pre-selection	▪ Requires high organizational effort ▪ High implementation costs
Fund of funds	Investment in VC funds managed by external venture capitalists	Y	High	High	▪ Continuous participation in deal-flow of VC ▪ Established trust through collaboration with VC	▪ Dependency on investment managers and funds ▪ High financial commitment
External scouting partner	Scouting by external service provider	N	High	Very high	▪ Professional service provided by experts	▪ High costs ▪ Knowledge loss due to communication
Scouting satellite	Scouting department located in startup "hot-spots"	Y	Very high	Very high	▪ Creation of network effects to startup ecosystem ▪ Intensive pre-selection	▪ High implementation costs ▪ Knowledge loss due to communication

Push instruments

					Advantages	Disadvantages
Networking with business partners	Communication of potentially interesting startups by business partners can be suppliers, consulting firms, VCs	N	Very low	Moderate	• Low implementation costs • Synergies regarding, e.g., industrialization	• Dependent on established network
Network with universities research institutes	Potentially interesting spin-off firms are communicated by universities or research institutes	N	Low	High	• Identification of startups in an early stage • Low implementation costs	• Dependent on established network
Network with non-partnering firms	Building a network with competitors, customers, and cross-industry parties	N	Low	Moderate	• Low implementation costs • Exchange of distant knowledge	• Knowledge sharing might be limited • Interest conflicts
E-mail, landing-, and web-page	Online contact opportunity for startups	N	Low	Low	• Low implementation costs • Complementary marketing effect	• No pre-selection • Resource-intensive selection

3.5. Discussion

Our study examines (1) organizational structures and (2) the implementation of search for startups within corporations. In the following, we discuss our findings under the light of boundary spanning and external knowledge sourcing literature.

To start with, the four identified approaches to organize the search for startups differ regarding the involvement of internal stakeholders and their closeness to the ordinary organization. One of the approaches describes an external, centrally organized unit, e.g., an overseas scouting (Monteiro & Birkinshaw, 2017) or CVC unit (Wadhwa & Basu, 2013). Our findings highlight difficulties in the knowledge transfer and boundary spanning for this approach due to missing links to the internal organization (Dushnitsky & Lenox, 2006; Rosenkopf & Nerkar, 2001). Further, internal centralized units also face the problem of missing intra-organizational links (Ancona & Caldwell, 1988, 1992). In contrast, internal, decentralized organizational structures limit possible constrains of not-invented here syndrome and missing absorptive capacity as project managers get to know startups and their ideas in an earlier stage (Cohen & Levinthal, 1990; Katz & Allen, 1982).

Regarding the implementation of search, the deducted process shows similarities to the identification and evaluation process for diversification opportunities deducted by Lichtenthaler (2005), which consists of search field definition, systematic search, and evaluation. Our results also provide more details explaining, e.g., the definition of search fields and application of tools compared to prior research (Rohrbeck, 2010). Further, we highlight a specific search process for external knowledge which extends prior findings on, e.g., individual search for inventions (Maggitti, Smith, & Katila, 2013) or general description of innovation processes on an organizational level (Salerno et al., 2015). In addition, we describe seven pull and four push instruments to realize the search for startups. Several of these have already been described in prior literature on external knowledge sourcing (Laursen & Salter, 2006; Leiponen & Helfat, 2010). Searching within databases or the internet as well as attending trade fairs and exhibitions have been described as sources of external knowledge (Cruz-González, López-Sáez, Navas-López, & Delgado-Verde, 2015; Leiponen & Helfat, 2010). Further, the establishment of networks to universities or research institutes as well as competitors (non-partnering firms) originates the same literature stream (Laursen, Masciarelli, & Prencipe, 2012; Laursen & Salter, 2014). Additional deal-flow can be provided by networks to business partner, such as suppliers, consulting firms, or venture capitalist. Networks to venture capitalist can be enhanced by investments in their funds, commonly referred to as fund of funds (Dushnitsky & Lenox, 2005; Monteiro et al., 2017). Literature has also described internal and external technology scouts (Rohrbeck, 2010; Wolff, 1992). Especially, external scouting entities, e.g., listening post, are effective approaches to access knowledge provided by startups (Gassmann & Gaso, 2004; Monteiro & Birkinshaw, 2017). Innovation contests have been discussed in literature (Boudreau, Lacetera, & Lakhani, 2011; Felin & Zenger, 2014). This approach to access external knowledge is very similar to self-organized pitch events as both require commitment and action of the external partner. Finally, startups can directly contact corporates via open channels, such as a corporate homepage. Thereby, startups follow a similar path as if applying for corporate engagement programs, such as accelerators (Kohler, 2016).

3.5.1. Theoretical contributions

Our research contributes to three major literature streams: external knowledge sourcing, boundary spanning, and the intersection of innovation management and purchasing. First, our research adds to the external innovation sourcing literature by addressing startups as corporations' future innovation partners (Weiblen & Chesbrough, 2015; Zaremba et al., 2016). While prior literature has primarily focused on established partners within the supply chain (Johnsen, 2009; Schiele, 2010), our study addresses the role of startups as providers of external ideas. Most scholars have focused on various external sources of knowledge, such as suppliers, customers, universities, or competitors (Criscuolo et al., 2018; Laursen & Salter, 2006). Just recently, the process to identify single sources of knowledge has been regarded in detail (Monteiro & Birkinshaw, 2017). Moreover, our findings provide 11 instruments to identify startups. As a consequence, our research adds to literature on open innovation instruments which allow firms to access external knowledge in a structured way (Homfeldt et al., 2017).

Second, we highlight four organizational structures showing how corporate organizations realize boundary spanning to access knowledge provided by startups (Rosenkopf & Almeida, 2003; Rosenkopf & Nerkar, 2001). These approaches allow corporations to link to the external knowledge providers (Basu et al., 2016; Souitaris, Zerbinati, & Liu, 2012). Whereas prior studies have focused on external scouting units embedded in local startup environments (Doz, Santos, & Williamson, 2001; Gassmann & Gaso, 2004), we highlight three internal approaches to organize the search for startups. Our findings are in line with recent research emphasizing the importance of close ties to internal organizational units (Monteiro & Birkinshaw, 2017).

Third, our findings add to literature on the intersection of innovation management and purchasing. As the study focuses on supply chain relationships between established firms and startups, we help to advance an understudied field (Kickul et al., 2011; Zaremba et al., 2017). We indicate how corporate firms identify innovative partners outside their networks and extend the limitations of prior research exclusively considering the identification of established partners (Pulles et al., 2014; Schiele, 2006). By showing how purchasing departments contribute to the search for startups, we support prior findings on the role of purchasing in the innovation process of corporate organizations (Schoenherr & Wagner, 2016; Wagner, 2012).

3.5.2. Managerial contributions

Digitalization and sharing economy are only two trends which now even affect product-focused industries, such as the automotive industry (Richter, Kraus, Brem, Durst, & Giselbrecht, 2017; Svahn et al., 2017). Consequently, existing technologies may become obsolete and the search for radical innovations with focus on digital products becomes a necessity. As startups often discover paths to face these challenges, managers should consider them as future partners (Anderson & Tushman, 1990; Bergek et al., 2013). Our study provides four organizational structures that are used to organize scouting for startups. When selecting one of these approaches, managers should consider costs and efforts of their implementation. In order to operationalize search for startups, managers can select of a set of instruments that are highlighted in our study. Further, the described process provides the basis for implementing structured search for startups.

3.5.3. Limitations and future research

Our research has limitations as findings may be specific to the automotive industry. However, "they might also be applicable to industries that have similar structural characteristics such as the aircraft, aircraft engine, semiconductor, medical device and consumer products industries" (Hüttinger et al., 2014, p. 713). Moreover, our case study is limited to a set of eight cases. As this study has explorative character, we were not able to evaluate which search approaches are most successful. Future studies could regard this from two ankles. On the one hand, an analysis of the impact of different organizational settings (internal/external and centralized/decentralized) on the success of search for startups as well as on the innovation performance of firms would provide an important contribution. On the other hand, future research could focus on the effectiveness of search strategies. Are more intensive search and broader application of search instruments beneficial for the searching firm? Such studies would add to previous findings analyzing the effects of search breadth and depth on the firms' innovation performance (Laursen & Salter, 2006; Leiponen & Helfat, 2010). Also, our research is limited to the perspective of established firms. A further assessment of identification instruments could be obtained by taking the perspective of startups on how to identify future business partners. Moreover, an analysis on individual level could enhance our understanding of searching and scouting for startups, e.g., regarding the effects of "the presence of technology scouting units, and the adoption or involvement of different organizational structures in the external search process—on the success rate of development, identification, and integration of external knowledge" (Bogers et al., 2017, p. 14). As identifying startups is only the first step to set up collaborations, future research could examine how corporations engage with startups to participate in their knowledge and how startups may support corporations to manage ambidexterity by balancing exploration and exploitation (Tushman & O'Reilly, 1996; Weiblen & Chesbrough, 2015).

3.6. Conclusions

Our study shows how corporate organization design their search for startups. We identify four organizational approaches and eleven search instruments. Our findings advance external knowledge sourcing literature as we identify internal approaches to organize the search for startups and instruments enabling the search for startups. By showing how firms can identify partners outside their existing network, we advance the intersection of innovation and purchasing literature.

Chapter 4 – Searching for startups: Search strategies, search effectiveness and radical innovation capabilities

Abstract:

Startups have evolved to an important external knowledge source. Yet, what has been missing so far is an analysis of which search strategies lead to search success (i.e., the identification of adequate and value creating startups) and the effects of these search activities on the searching firms' radical innovation capability (i.e., the ability to generate innovations that significantly transform existing solutions). Our results show that searching broadly and intensively enhances successful search for startups. We further reveal a positive relationship between search success and firms' radical innovation capability. Thereby, we add to organizational learning literature by illustrating that organizations build explorative learning capabilities due to the stimuli accompanying the search for startups. By examining 11 search approaches in depths, we also provide insights for managers about the usefulness of distinct instruments. For instance, we find that startup pitch events best supports successful search for startups.

4.1. Introduction

Firms rely increasingly on external sources of knowledge and ideas beyond their boundaries (Criscuolo et al., 2018; van Wijk et al., 2008). External knowledge is important as it adds new variations of problem solutions that are unknown to the in-sourcing organization and thereby contributes to its combinatory search (Fleming & Sorenson, 2001; Katila & Ahuja, 2002; March, 1991). The literature on open innovation identifies various sources of external knowledge, such as suppliers, universities, customers, or competitors (Van de Vrande, 2013; West & Bogers, 2014). Recently, the role of startups as new innovative knowledge providers has received special attention (Linton & Solomon, 2017; Weiblen & Chesbrough, 2015; Zaremba et al., 2017). By engaging in partnerships with startups, firms aim to benefit from startups' characteristics, such as flexibility, alertness, creativity, and willingness to take risks (Criscuolo et al., 2012; Marion et al., 2012).

Considering the potential set of external knowledge sources, prior research has particularly investigated the identification of innovative suppliers in the firms' supply base (Pulles et al., 2014; Schiele, 2006), e.g., by applying competitions in the early stages of firms' innovation processes (Langner & Seidel, 2009). Only recently, scholars have begun to study how firms identify startups, but have so far limited their research to the design of external structures, which includes sensing or scouting units (Monteiro & Birkinshaw, 2017). All existing studies concerning the search for startups are either qualitative or describe only particular search approaches (Homfeldt et al., 2017; Weiblen & Chesbrough, 2015). Yet, we miss a broad quantitative study on how to best search for startups and which search strategies to apply in order to achieve successful search for startups. Hence, our first research question is: *Which search strategies lead to successful identification of startups?*

By accessing knowledge from startups, firms increase their innovation performance (Wadhwa et al., 2016). Minority investments (Dushnitsky & Lenox, 2006) or joint development projects (Gassmann et al., 2010) are the most commonly used approaches to participate in startups' knowledge when entering into the collaboration stage. Beyond the benefits related to the collaboration with startups, our knowledge about the effects of implementing structured search for startups is limited. Organizations theory shows that firms generate new knowledge by combining external stimuli with existing routines (Zollo & Winter, 2002). As a consequence, firms require continuous creative stimuli from their environment, which is achieved through being open to external knowledge (Colombo et al., 2017). In this study, we propose that the successful search for startups implies necessary external impulses to generate radical innovations and subsequently expand the firms' organizational capabilities. Thereby, startups may provide a considerable contribution to rejuvenate the organization. Accordingly, our second research question is: *What impact does successful search for startups have on the radical innovation capability of the sourcing firm?*

Based on an international sample of 97 predominantly large firms from different industries, such as automotive, manufacturing, and telecommunications, this article sheds light on the introduced gaps in previous research by investigating how firms can achieve successful search for startups and if there is subsequent influence on the searching firms' organizational capabilities. Thereby, we add to external knowledge sourcing literature by focusing on startups as an increasingly important source of innovation and address the gap in literature on the successful identification of partners beyond the existing supply base (Weiblen & Chesbrough, 2015; Zaremba et al., 2017). Further, our findings contribute to the literature on organizational learning and capabilities, as we explore whether the identification and discovery of promising startups and the assessment of their ideas provide creative stimuli for the sourcing organization (Colombo et al., 2017; O'Connor & De Martino, 2006). Finally, we show which search strategies are most effective for managers form various disciplines, such as R&D, corporate venturing, or procurement, and highlight the most powerful instruments.

The remainder of this article is structured as follows. First, we provide an overview of existing literature on external knowledge sourcing from startups as well as literature on organizational capabilities and learning, including the development of our hypotheses. Then, we illustrate the sample as well as the methodological approach. After reporting the results, we discuss our findings based on existing literature, highlight limitations, and show future research paths.

4.2. Theoretical background and hypotheses

4.2.1. External knowledge sourcing from startups

Theoretically, external knowledge sourcing is closely linked to the knowledge-based view of the firm and to organizational learning (Grant, 1996b; March, 1991). Kogut and Zander (1992, p. 391) state that innovation is related to firms' capabilities to "exploit its knowledge of the unexplored potential of technology" and "generate new combinations of existing knowledge". As a consequence, accessing external knowledge has long been seen as crucial to a firm's innovation success. Specifically, it is argued that external knowledge adds new variations of problem solutions that are unknown to the in-sourcing organization and thereby increases the chance to find novel linkages and to develop innovative products (Katila and Ahuja, 2002). Extensive research exists providing evidence on the relationship between openness to external knowledge and a firm's innovation performance (Lakemond et al., 2016; Leiponen & Helfat, 2010).

Various external partners have been established as important sources of innovation, particularly including customers, suppliers, universities, and competitors (Rothaermel, 2002; West & Bogers, 2014). However, in recent years, startups have increasingly received attention as a promising external source of innovation (Weiblen & Chesbrough, 2015; Zaremba et al., 2017), because they offer a unique set of capabilities that distinguish them from incumbent firms (Brunswicker & Hutschek, 2010; Gassmann et al., 2010). Startups, also referred to as new ventures, are firms that have not been in existence for a long time (usually with a maximum age of eight years) (Song et al., 2008). As startups miss assets, they cannot experiment with many different ideas, but have to focus on specific ideas (van Burg et al., 2012). Thus, new product development is more focused and dynamic within startups compared to more established organizations (Rothaermel, 2002). Further, startups apply customer-centric methods like design thinking or lean startup in order to support early interaction with customers. Through iterative testing of their ideas on the market, startups receive continuous feedback, which allows them to develop solutions that provide benefits to potential users (Blank, 2013; Weiblen & Chesbrough, 2015). To innovate is crucial for startups in order to quickly access market shares and early cash flows (Schoonhoven et al., 1990). Due to usual small firm size, startups can sustain high flexibility and short chains of command (Kickul et al., 2011; Rothaermel, 2002). As a consequence, startups do not follow dedicated routines that often represents a barrier to innovation. Instead of having already established structures and languorous processes, startup processes are nascent and yield novel outcomes (Baker et al., 2003; Katila & Shane, 2005). Finally, startups possess high willingness to take risks and high growth potential, which allows to accomplish a prime position for innovation, especially radical innovation (Criscuolo et al., 2012; Engel, 2011). Overall, this innovative potential of startups is a highly attractive feature and makes them interesting innovation partners for in-sourcing organizations.

4.2.2. Search instruments to identify startups

Given the promising merits of startups' knowledge and ideas, different ways of how to identify startups in the early stages of a firm's innovation process have received increasing interest among scholars and practitioners, for example exploring the role of (technology) scouts in detail (Pauwels et al., 2016; Rohrbeck, 2010). In particular, the search for startups through new instruments has received attention since the identification of startups needs, in contrast to established partners such as suppliers, a radically different approach given non-established relations to the searching firm. Our literature review yielded eleven different search instruments (see Table 8), which either demand distinct actions (active search) or are rather passive.

Table 8: Summary of search instruments

	Description	*References*
Desk research	Manual web-based search, automatic web screening and external database services	Cruz-González et al. (2015); Leiponen and Helfat (2010)
Scientific conferences/ publications	Visits of scientific conferences, reviewing publications	Cruz-González et al. (2015); Leiponen and Helfat (2010)
Trade fairs/ exhibitions	Visits of trade fairs and exhibitions	Cruz-González et al. (2015); Leiponen and Helfat (2010)
Self-organized pitch events	Organizing startup events with open registration or professional search and pre-selection	Homfeldt et al. (2017); Weiblen and Chesbrough (2015)
Fund of funds	Investment in VC funds managed by external venture capitalists	Monteiro et al. (2017)
External scouting partner	Scouting by external service provider	Rohrbeck (2010)
Scouting satellite	Scouting department located in startup "hot-spots"	Monteiro and Birkinshaw (2017)
Networking with business partners	Communication of potentially interesting startups by business partners can be suppliers, consulting firms, VCs	Monteiro et al. (2017)
Network with universities/ research institutes	Potentially interesting spin-off firms are communicated by universities or research institutes	Cruz-González et al. (2015); Leiponen and Helfat (2010)
Network with non-partnering firms	Building a network with competitors, customers, and cross-industry parties	Cruz-González et al. (2015); Leiponen and Helfat (2010)
E-mail, landing-, and web-page	Online contact opportunity for startups	Kohler (2016)

Regarding active approaches, startups can be identified through manual web-based search, the automatic screening of startup databases, or visits of scientific conferences and public trade fairs (Cruz-González et al., 2015; Leiponen & Helfat, 2010). In addition, organizations can organize pitch events during which startups have to present their ideas in front of experts (Homfeldt et al., 2017; Weiblen & Chesbrough, 2015). Another approach is the investment in funds that allow the investing organization to participate in the deal flow of venture capitalists (VCs) (Monteiro et al., 2017). Moreover, the identification of startups can be actively managed by the support of external scouting partners (Rohrbeck, 2010) or scouting satellites, which describe scouting departments located in startup "hot-spots" (Monteiro & Birkinshaw, 2017). Apart from actively managed identification instruments, literature highlights networks to business partners (e.g., VCs or consulting firms), universities, and even non-partnering firms (e.g., competitors) as sources for the identification of startups without actively searching (Cruz-González et al., 2015; Leiponen & Helfat, 2010; Monteiro et al., 2017). Finally, startups can directly address the organization if firms offer an open contact platform, such as a homepage or mailing address (Kohler, 2016).

4.2.3. Search strategies for the successful identification of startups

Defining the search scope, prior research has focused on search breadth and search depth (Katila & Ahuja, 2002; Laursen & Salter, 2006). Laursen and Salter (2006, p. 131) introduced the concept of external search breadth and depth as "two components of the openness of individual firms' external search strategies". Search breadth has been defined as "the number of external search channels that firms rely upon in their innovative activity", while search depth is referred to as "the extent to which firms draw deeply from the different external sources or search channels" (Laursen & Salter, 2006, p. 134 f.). There are manifold studies in the open innovation literature using these constructs (Y. Chen et al., 2016; Criscuolo et al., 2018; Laursen & Salter, 2006). Leiponen and Helfat (2010) indicate a positive relationship between search breadth and innovation success, which is also confirmed by Monteiro et al. (2017). Other studies show positive effects of search depth on incremental innovation (Chiang & Hung, 2010). Both, search breadth and search depth have been associated with radical innovation and thus successful search for distant external knowledge (Chiang & Hung, 2010; Laursen & Salter, 2006).

Exploratory organizational learning is described as learning based on a broad and general search for knowledge and may lead to more variations, flexibility, and innovations (Levinthal & March, 1993; March, 1991). Hence, expanding firm´s knowledge stock by accessing a large number of search channels will allow a firm to search successfully. Also economic models have shown the success of 'parallel path strategy', which is described as the conduction of multiple parallel searches (Baldwin & Clark, 2000; Nelson, 1961). These models illustrate that the "greater the number of draws from the distribution, the more likely it is that one of the draws will exceed the critical valued needed" (Leiponen & Helfat, 2010, p. 225). We transfer these arguments to our object of investigation. Accordingly, we argue that pursuing a greater number of startup search approaches increases the chance that one of these approaches leads to search success, which we define as the identification of sufficient, adequate, and value generating startups. Hence, we propose that:

Hypothesis 1 (H1):   *Search breadth is positively related to search success for startups.*

Further, we follow the argumentation of Laursen and Salter (2006, p. 136) that the intensive use of search channels is important to establish constant exchange and collaborations with external partners. Due to high degree of discontinuity, only specific sources and channels may be important (Utterback & Abernathy, 1975). As proposed by the literature on social networks and social capital, strong and frequent contacts with specific knowledge sources supports in-depth and fine-grained knowledge access and flow (Dyer & Nobeoka, 2000; Leana & Van Buren, 1999). Thus, more focused search will lead to higher search success, which allows us to derive the following hypothesis:

Hypothesis 2 (H2):   *Search depth is positively related to search success for startups.*

4.2.4. Organizational capabilities and the ability to generate radical innovations

Establishing and extending organizational capabilities is essential for firms to grow (Dosi, Faillo, & Marengo, 2008; Penrose, 1959). According to Zander and Kogut (1995, p. 76), organizational capabilities are defined as the "organizing principles by which individual and functional expertise is structured, coordinated, and communicated". The organizational capability to innovate (innovation capability) allows firms to accumulate, connect, and transform different types of knowledge in order to generate new solutions (Lawson & Samson, 2001). Innovation capabilities concern competences and expertise related to new product creation and introduction (Hagedoorn & Duysters, 2002). While incremental innovation capabilities provide only minimal differences to existing knowledge and routines, radical innovation capabilities allow to expand existing knowledge drastically. Radical innovation capabilities allow organizations to create new-to-the-world products with high customer benefit and therefore are the source of competitive advantage (Chandy & Tellis, 1998, 2000). Subramaniam and Youndt (2005, p. 452) define a firm's radical innovation capability as "the capability to generate innovations that significantly transform existing products and services." In doing so, firms fundamentally change the technological path and existing organizational capabilities by generating new knowledge departing from existing skills (March, 1991).

Especially, established firms under-invest in the realization of truly novel ideas because these mature organizations face inertia of prior investments (Henderson, 1993). Prior experience and accumulated learning limit the success of established firms' distant search and generation of radical innovations (Christensen, 1997) caused by existing routines (Levinthal & March, 1993), structures (O'Connor & Rice, 2013), and mental models (Tripsas & Gavetti, 2000). To overcome these restrictions and generate organizational knowledge, firms have to combine external stimuli with existing routines (Zollo & Winter, 2002). Thus, organizations rely on continuous creative stimuli and are forced to develop openness capabilities (Colombo et al., 2017; O'Connor & De Martino, 2006).

By contrast, startups are powerful engines of radical innovations, because they are not limited by myopia and inertia (Levinthal & March, 1993). Indeed, startups possess characteristics that allow them to generate necessary stimuli for radical innovations (Criscuolo et al., 2012; Marion et al., 2012). Prior studies have shown that the knowledge provided by startups increases the in-sourcing organizations' innovation performance (Dushnitsky & Lenox, 2006; Wadhwa et al., 2016). In addition, Love, Roper, and Vahter (2014) identify learning processes through the identification of partner firms and the development of routines to interact with them. Their study also finds evidence that management teams benefit from identifying, selecting, and interacting with external partners over time. Thus, the engagement in structured search for knowledge from startups may provide the relevant stimuli to succeed at generating fundamentally new solutions. Taking the described possibilities for organizational learning into account, we propose the following hypothesis:

Hypothesis 3 (H3):   *Search success for startups is positively related to the firm's radical innovation capability.*

4.3. Method

4.3.1. Data collection and sample

To test our hypotheses on a profound empirical basis, we surveyed a cross-industry sample by means of a self-administered internet-based survey. When collecting the data, we were faced with the challenge of investigating a topic that is in its infancy while at the same time addressing representative firms that were able to provide meaningful information. To achieve this, we collaborated with a large international venture capital and scouting firm that supported the distribution of our survey among its business networks consisting of firms that actively managed corporate-startup relationships and especially the search for startups. Based on the key informant approach, managers that are responsible for the identification of startups were addressed (John & Reve, 1982). In exchange for their participation, respondents were offered a summary of the results. The sampling approach resulted in 97 usable responses with complete information on our key research constructs. This represents a response rate of 19.0% using 511 visiting firms to the survey site as the population size, common practice in online survey studies (Balka, Raasch, & Herstatt, 2014; Schweisfurth, 2017). The response rate is comparable to prior studies concerning the search for external knowledge and firm's radical innovation performance (Y.-C. Chang, Chang, Chi, Chen, & Deng, 2012; Martini, Neirotti, & Appio, 2017). Since we contacted a very specific informant group, the relatively small sample size is acceptable.

Our sample consists of firms mainly belonging to the automotive (21.6%), manufacturing (12.4%), healthcare (5.2%), and telecommunication (14.4%) industry. Further, we addressed primarily large multi-national corporations, since 42.5% of firms in our sample have more than 5,000 employees. Annual revenues were above 500 million USD for 63.7% of the firms in our sample, more than one quarter stated to have more than 5 billion USD of annual revenues. Most of the respondents belong to the board of management or were top managers, as more than 50% of the respondents were above senior management level.

We tested for non-response bias by comparing the early (first 10%) to last (last 10 %) of responses (Armstrong & Overton, 1977). As the t-test of our independent and dependent variables showed no significant difference ($p > 0.10$), we conclude that non-response bias does not pose a significant threat to the validity our results.

4.3.2. Survey instrument and measures

The survey and its measures were developed through several stages respecting standard techniques (Dillman, 2006). Accordingly, a preliminary questionnaire was drafted on the basis of the reviewed literature and interviews with practitioners, such as two experts from a venture capitalist and two innovation managers from a large automotive manufacturer. For the most part, we were able to draw on scales that had been validated in prior studies. However, in order to fit the original scales to our specific context, it was necessary to modify several items. We also paid particular attention that our survey design maintained the interest of the respondents to the end of the survey and limited burden on respondents. The survey instrument was discussed with ten scholars and practitioners with expertise in the area of innovation management and their feedback was incorporated into the survey.

Dependent variables

Following previous discussions on innovation capabilities, Subramaniam and Youndt (2005) developed a measure for an organization's *radical innovation capability* that is defined as the capability to generate innovations that significantly transform existing solutions. We used an extended four-item version of this construct employed by Menguc et al. (2014) (Cronbach's α = 0.78). The respondents were asked to rate the firm's capability of generating radical innovations relative to the main competitors by considering the extent to which the generated innovations in new products differ substantially from existing solutions and significantly enhance customers' product experiences. Our measure for *search success* is adapted from Kock, Heising, and Gemünden (2015), who originally developed the scale to assess a firm's front-end success concerning the identification and generation of promising ideas. We modified the items in order to fit the original scale to our specific context. Accordingly, the respondents were asked to assess the firm's success regarding the identification of sufficient, adequate, and value creating startups (five items, Cronbach's α = 0.80). All items were measured with a 5-point Likert scale. The exact wording of the scales is presented in Appendix Table 16. Search success serves as the independent variable in Hypothesis 3 as well. Further independent variables are introduced in the following.

Independent variables

Search breadth and *search depth* have been measured in open innovation previously by simply adding up the usage and extend of usage of various sources of knowledge (Laursen & Salter, 2006, 2014; Leiponen & Helfat, 2010). We adapted this kind of measurement to our object of investigation. Our survey listed eleven search instruments, such as self-organized pitch events or networking with business partners. Respondents were asked to indicate on a Likert-type scale how intensively they apply each of the instruments. A '0' indicated that the firm did not use the respective instrument, while a '5' indicated that the instrument was very intensively used by the firm. The selected search instruments were deducted from the literature (see section 2.2) and approved for completeness and clarity by discussions with overall 13 experts from eight different firms with main business in the automotive industry. Among the experts were managing directors of corporate venture units as well as managers within strategy, innovation management, and procurement. The instruments used in the survey are shown in Table 8.

Search breadth was measured as the sum of instruments used by the responding firms ranging from 0 to 11. First, each of the eleven instruments was coded as a binary variable, 0 being not applied and 1 being applied to any extend. Subsequently, the eleven instruments were added up so that each firm received a value of 0 when none of the search instruments was used, while the firm received the value 11, when all instruments were in use. In the case of *search depth,* we applied a similar procedure, but took account of how intensively a search instrument was used by the firm. Specifically, a survey response of either 4 ("intensively used") or 5 ("very intensively used") received a binary value of 1; survey responses below (scores 0 - 3) received a binary value of 0. As in the case of search breadth, the final measure for search depth was obtained by adding these binary variables, whose result is an index informing with how many search instruments a firm intensively search for startups (see Cruz-González et al., 2015; Laursen & Salter, 2006, 2014; Leiponen & Helfat, 2010 for similar measurement).

Control variables
We used several control variables to preclude undesirable sources of variance in the hypothesis tests, e.g., firm-specifics. First, *firm size* is a broadly used control variable in studies related to innovation (Ahuja & Katila, 2001; Laursen & Salter, 2014). Larger firms possess more resources, which may allow them to search more intensively for startups and establish more powerful R&D centers. To enhance simplicity of our survey, we allowed the respondents to select from five different options: 1 = "< 50", 2 = "51 – 100", 3 = "101 – 1000", 4 = "1001 – 5000", 5 = "> 5000" (cf. Gao, Xie, & Zhou, 2015). Second, we included *R&D intensity* as a control variable (cf. Laursen and Salter, 2006). We measured R&D intensity in percent and provided this definition: "ratio of annual expenditure for R&D to annual revenues". Third, we controlled for *industry* by developing a set of five dummy variables. The industry dummy displays various environmental dimensions, including competition and technological opportunity (Veugelers, 1997).

Common method variance
As our employed data is of self-reported nature, we suggest the potential threat of common method variance to the validity of our results. Following prior recommendations (Podsakoff, MacKenzie, Lee, & Podsakoff, 2003), we inserted various measures to counteract the potential problem of common method bias in our data. We applied ex ante remedies that concern the

design of the research, e.g., the administration of the questionnaire or the survey design, as well as ex post remedies after the responses were collected (S.-J. Chang, Van Witteloostuijn, & Eden, 2010). With regard to the design of our research, the survey provided only general information about the study's objectives, but no clues about the actual relationships under investigation. Specifically, our question design did not allow to easily understand which relationships were studied, as search breadth and search depth are measured as an additive index. As a consequence, we established difficult-to-visualize relationships between our dependent and independent variables. Furthermore, we offered anonymity and confidentiality for the respondents to reduce social desirability bias in the responses. In addition to the ex ante remedies, we conducted a latent factor analysis, which is equivalent to Harman's single factor test (Harman, 1976). As the highest emerging factor was 19.8% and six components had eigenvalues greater than 1.0, no single factor constituted for a large proportion of the total variance. In addition to the Harman's single-factor approach, we applied the unmeasured latent methods factor test (Liang, Saraf, Hu, & Xue, 2007; Perols, Zimmermann, & Kortmann, 2013; Podsakoff et al., 2003). Table 9 illustrates the results.

Table 9: Results of latent factor loadings analysis

	CL	CL^2	t_{CL}	MFL	MFL^2	t_{MFL}
SB	1.000	1.000	0.000	0.000	0.000	0.000
SD	1.000	1.000	0.000	0.000	0.000	0.000
SE1	0.552	0.305	3.855	0.210	0.044	1.405
SE2	1.019	1.038	7.517	-0.296	0.088	1.861
SE3	0.966	0.933	6.822	-0.184	0.034	1.398
SE4	0.562	0316	3.263	0.204	0.042	1.274
SE5	0.646	0.417	3.446	0.075	0.006	0.383
RAD1	0.915	0.837	11.772	-0.117	0.014	1.230
RAD2	0.955	0.912	14.743	-0.147	0.022	1.643
RAD3	0.658	0.433	3.824	0.089	0.008	0.497
RAD4	0.551	0.304	3.638	0.215	0.046	1.648
Mean	0.802	0.681	5.353	0.004	0.027	1.031

$N = 97$.
SB = Search breadth; SD = Search depth; SE = Search success; RAD = Radical innovation capability;
CL= Construct Loading; MFL= Method Factor Loading.
t >1.96 = significant path at p < 0.05 (two-sided).

As a first step, we generated a latent "common factor" that covered all principal constructs' indicators. Then we estimated the average substantive variance described as the loading between the main construct and the indicator construct as well as the average method-based variance, which stands for the loading of the common factor on the indicator constructs. While the substantive variance is on average 0.681, the average method-based variance is 0.027. Hence, the ratio of substantive variance to method variance is about 25:1 and thus substantive variance is considerably greater than method variance. Further, all of the method factor loadings are insignificant ($p > 0.05$). In sum, both tests indicate that common method variance should not be a problem in our study.

4.4. Analysis and results

4.4.1. Descriptive data

Descriptive statistics and correlations for all variables are provided in Table 10. The mean of search breadth represents how many search instruments are in place at the investigated firms, while the mean of search depth shows the number of search instruments with intensive use. With a maximum of eleven search instruments, the mean of search breadth is overall very high (9.48), while the mean for search depth is only 3.57. This shows that firms apply many search instruments but only a few intensively with the highest values for networking with business partners (mean = 3.21), desk research (mean = 3.16), and networking with universities/research institutes (mean = 3.09). Similar to prior studies (Cruz-González et al., 2015; Laursen & Salter, 2006), we find a high correlation of search breadth and search depth, which supports our assumption that both search breadth and depth are complementary.

Table 10: Descriptives and correlations

	Variable	Mean	SD	1	2	3	4	5	6
1	Firm size	3.49	1.57						
2	R&D intensity	9.56	9.87	-0.323**					
3	Search breadth	9.48	2.03	0.115	0.169				
4	Search depth	3.57	2.53	-0.037	-0.041	0.408***			
5	Search success	3.23	0.79	-0.115	0.204+	0.458***	0.437***		
6	Radical Innovation capability	3.25	0.72	-0.276*	0.113	0.161	0.384***	0.371***	

$N = 97$, except for firm size ($N = 80$) and R&D intensity ($N = 74$).
$^+ p < 0.1$, $^* p < 0.05$, $^{**} p < 0.01$, $^{***} p < 0.001$.

4.4.2. Regression results

To test our hypotheses, we applied OLS regression. Our dataset consists of 97 usable cases for our dependent and independent variables. However, for some of the control variables we have missing values leading to 74 cases without any missing values (dependent, independent, and control variables). To deal with the problem of missing values, we ran our models both with listwise exclusion and mean imputation in case of missing data (see Schafer & Graham, 2002). Collinearity statistics calculated for all regression analyses did not indicate problematic levels of multi-collinearity. All VIFs (based on standardized variables) did not exceed 1.8 and thus were below the critical value of 10. Therefore, we follow that multicollinearity did not strain our results (Kutner, Nachtsheim, & Neter, 2004). Further, no obvious outliers were detected and residuals appeared to be normally distributed (Hair, Black, Babin, Anderson, & Tatham, 2006).

The regression results are shown in Table 11 and Table 12. In the following, we report the results for the reduced and complete sample ($N = 74$). In Model 1 and 2, the dependent variable is *search success* (Hypotheses 1 and 2), whereas in Model 3 and 4, *radical innovation capability* is the dependent variable (Hypothesis 3). Model 1 and 3 only contain the control variables. In Model 2, we add *search breadth* and *search depth* as independent variables. Regression model 4 adds *search success* as independent variable. Model 3 and 4 show a good fit as indicated by the high significance of F values and the increase of R^2 by 20.8% from Model 1 to 2 as well as the change of R^2 by 8.8% from Model 3 to 4. Model 2 shows positive and significant relationship of search breadth ($\beta = 0.201$, $p < 0.1$) and search depth ($\beta = 0.356$, $p < 0.01$) with the dependent variable search success. Thus, we can confirm Hypotheses 1 and 2. Further, in Model 4 search success is significant and positively associated with radical innovation capability ($\beta = 0.312$, $p < 0.01$), thus providing support for Hypothesis 3. As illustrated in Table 12, similar results were obtained in case of mean imputation for missing data (N = 97). Search breadth shows even slightly higher significance, while search depth as well as search success remain at the same significance level.

Table 11: Results of OLS regression analysis ($N = 74$)

	Hypotheses	Dependent variable: Search success		Dependent variable: Radical innovation capability	
		Model 1 (Controls)	Model 2 (Effects)	Model 3 (Controls)	Model 4 (Effects)
(Constant)		2.952***	1.832***	3.326***	2.480***
		(0.324)	(0.470)	(0.273)	(0.387)
Firm size		0.061	-0.015	-0.224	-0.243+
		(0.077)	(0.070)	(0.065)	(0.061)
R&D intensity		0.219+	0.188	0.112	0.043
		(0.010)	(0.010)	(0.009)	(0.008)
Automotive		-0.084	0.008	0.022	0.048
		(0.270)	(0.244)	(0.228)	(0.216)
Manufacturing		-0.084	-0.113	0.305*	0.331**
		(0.298)	(0.268)	(0.251)	(0.239)
Healthcare		-0.041	-0.036	-0.053	-0.040
		(0.395)	(0.355)	(0.333)	(0.316)
Telecommunication		0.195	0.207+	0.321**	0.260*
		(0.278)	(0.248)	(0.235)	(0.226)
Search breadth	H1		0.201+		
			(0.050)		
Search depth	H2		0.356**		
			(0.040)		
Search success	H3				0.312**
					(0.098)
R^2		0.097	0.305	0.238	0.326
adjusted R^2		0.016	0.220	0.169	0.254
change R^2		0.097	0.208	0.238	0.088
F value		1.199	3.573**	3.482**	4.555***
change F value		1.199	9.754	3.482	8.619

Coefficient estimates of OLS regression with standard errors (in parentheses) are shown. Reported estimates refer to standardized coefficients. Baseline category for *industry* is "other".
$^+ p < 0.1$, $^* p < 0.05$, $^{**} p < 0.01$, $^{***} p < 0.001$.

Table 12: Results of OLS regression analysis ($N = 97$)

	Hypotheses	Dependent variable: Search success		Dependent variable: Radical innovation capability	
		Model 1 (Controls)	Model 2 (Effects)	Model 3 (Controls)	Model 4 (Effects)
(Constant)		2.963***	1.660***	3.355***	2.469***
		(0.291)	(0.371)	(0.255)	(0.354)
Firm size		0.049	-0.017	-0.138	-0.154
		(0.068)	(0.078)	(0.060)	(0.056)
R&D intensity		0.192+	0.146	0.096	0.033
		(0.010)	(0.009)	(0.009)	(0.009)
Automotive		-0.078	-0.011	-0.101	-0.075
		(0.228)	(0.196)	(0.200)	(0.190)
Manufacturing		-0.053	-0.116	0.189+	0.206*
		(0.260)	(0.225)	(0.228)	(0.216)
Healthcare		-0.036	-0.034	-0.085	-0.073
		(0.382)	(0.328)	(0.335)	(0.317)
Telecommunication		0.194+	0.159+	0.216*	0.153
		(0.246)	(0.218)	(0.216)	(0.208)
Search breadth	H1		0.299**		
			(0.038)		
Search depth	H2		0.338**		
			(0.030)		
Search success	H3				0.326**
					(0.087)
R^2		0.081	0.354	0.158	0.256
adjusted R^2		0.020	0.295	0.102	0.197
change R^2		0.081	0.273	0.158	0.098
F value		1.321	6.028***	2.817*	4.372***
change F value		1.321	18.598	2.817	11.696

Coefficient estimates of OLS regression with standard errors (in parentheses) are shown. Reported estimates refer to standardized coefficients. Baseline category for *industry* is "other".
+$p < 0.1$, *$p < 0.05$, **$p < 0.01$, ***$p < 0.001$.

4.4.3. Robustness checks

As to our small sample size, we applied percentile bootstrapping, which uses resamples to iteratively estimate the coefficients. In doing so, we prevent that our results are dependent on existing outliers within our dataset (Efron & Tibshirani, 1994). The results using 5,000 resamples confirmed our findings. Similar results were obtained with different resample sizes (500, 1,000, 2,000, 3,000 and 4,000). Furthermore, we confirmed our findings by applying the PLS (partial least squares) algorithm, which is recommended for small sample sizes with less than 250 observations (Reinartz, Haenlein, & Henseler, 2009). Again, this yielded similar results, further confirming the robustness of our findings. In addition, we replaced the control variable firm size with annual revenues as an alternative measure (selection of one of the following five items: 1 = "under \$200M", 2 = "\$200M – \$500M", 3 = "\$500M – \$1B", 4 = "\$1B – \$5B", and 5 = "above \$5B"). Results remained robust, even after including both firm size and annual revenues as control variables.

As several prior studies describe non-linear relationships for search breadth and depth (Katila & Ahuja, 2002; Laursen & Salter, 2006, 2014), we analyzed our data for quadratic effects. We conducted a polynomial regression to analyze the effects (Shanock, Baran, Gentry, Pattison, & Heggestad, 2010). The results did not show any curvilinear effects ($p > 0.10$). Figure 5 illustrates the surface analysis of search breadth and search depth regarding their influence on search success.

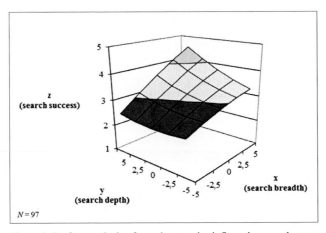

Figure 5: Surface analysis of search strategies influencing search success

4.5. Discussion and implications

In seeking to shed light on external knowledge sourcing from startups, this paper provides first empirical evidence for positive effects of open search strategies concerning the identification of startups and the subsequent benefits for the searching firms' radical innovation capability. Our findings illustrate that broad and intensive search allows firms to successfully identify startups and that this search activities enhance firms' radical innovation capability. In the following, we discuss our findings considering literature on organizational learning and organizational capabilities as well as external knowledge sourcing.

The results of various studies show a curvilinear relationship between search activities and innovation performance. This inverted U-shape is broadly explained as a result of "over-search" since absorptive capacity of firms is limited and does not allow to transfer infinite external knowledge (Cohen & Levinthal, 1990; Köhler, Sofka, & Grimpe, 2012; Laursen & Salter, 2006). Various studies analyzing external sources of knowledge and their impact on innovation performance confirm this reasoning (Rothaermel & Alexandre, 2009; Wadhwa et al., 2016). By contrast, our study focuses on the effects of search breadth and depth on the outcome of search. Thus, over-searching is not an issue in this context. A further reason might lay in the difference of our construct. The analysis concerns search success as a dependent variable, which is a less complex construct than innovation performance. We see especially difficulties in transferring ideas into organizations, e.g., due to limited absorptive capacity (Cohen & Levinthal, 1990). This effect applies to innovation performance, but does not influence search success and thus confirms our hypotheses.

Similar to prior findings, our descriptive results show that search depth is much less common than search breadth (J. Chen, Chen, & Vanhaverbeke, 2011; Chiang & Hung, 2010; Laursen & Salter, 2006). Resource constraints may limit firms to intensively apply many search instruments. We observe that the firms in our sample make use of various search instruments, but focus on specific ones in depths. Consequently, our sample firms follow parallel search strategies in combination with strong and frequent application of specific search instruments.

To develop radical innovation capabilities, firms must be able to support three processes: discovery, incubation, and acceleration (O'Connor & Ayers, 2005; O'Connor & De Martino, 2006). The search for startups supports especially the explorative phase of discovery. Our findings show that successful search and the generation of a powerful startup portfolio increases firms' radical innovation capability as startups provide powerful and innovative ideas. Further, the continuous screening and evaluation of radical ideas may enable the organization to follow new explorative path and lead to more variation as well as new customer value (March, 1991).

4.5.1. Theoretical implications

Our findings add to the literature on external knowledge sourcing and open innovation by focusing on startups as an increasingly important external source of innovation (Weiblen & Chesbrough, 2015; Zaremba et al., 2017). We extend prior findings limited to search for various external knowledge sources (Criscuolo et al., 2018; Laursen & Salter, 2006) or other external partners, such as suppliers (Pulles et al., 2014; Schiele, 2006) or lead users (Bilgram, Brem, & Voigt, 2008). Our findings highlight that broad and intensive search lead to higher search success. Thus, we are able to transfer the frequently applied measurement for search strategies to a new context compared to prior analyses with focus on internal search for knowledge or search for external knowledge among many sources (Katila & Ahuja, 2002; Laursen & Salter, 2006).

We further show that distant knowledge, which is inherent in startups, provides additional new variations of knowledge and explorative ideas to solve existing problems (Katila & Ahuja, 2002; March, 1991). The acquisition and application of external knowledge contributes to firms renewal and the extension of their capabilities (Agarwal & Helfat, 2009; Eisenhardt & Martin, 2000). Knowledge from startups is one source of necessary external stimuli that allows, in combination with existing knowledge, the generation of new knowledge (Fleming & Sorenson, 2001; Katila & Ahuja, 2002). Contrary to prior research, which has only shown positive effects of collaborations on firm's innovation performance (Laursen & Salter, 2006), we analyze the outcome of search activities on firms' capabilities. As stated in prior research, external creative stimuli are a prerequisite to generate radical innovations (Colombo et al., 2017; O'Connor & De Martino, 2006). Our findings indicate that the discovery of novel startups and the assessment of their ideas in the early stages of a firm's innovation process ensures such constant external stimuli. Overall, we show how a very specific identification process for external partners contributes to organizational learning and helps to expand organizational capabilities.

In addition, we show that firms start building own explorative learning capabilities as a consequence of constantly dealing with external radical innovations provided by startups. Thus, our study contributes to ambidexterity literature by illustrating a way for organizations to expand their explorative capabilities by continuously learning from external partners. Similar to prior research, our findings underline the benefits of exploration via externally oriented modes (Stettner & Lavie, 2014). In particular, firms enrich their knowledge bases by establishing ties to new partners without prior business relations such as startups (Lavie & Rosenkopf, 2006). Our results reveal that the search for startups provides the necessary impulse for firms to follow explorative learning (Levinthal & March, 1993; March, 1991).

Finally, our findings also add to literature on the intersection of innovation management and operations management (Kickul et al., 2011; Zaremba et al., 2017). We indicate how firms successfully search for innovative partners outside their established networks and extend the limitations of prior research exclusively considering the identification of established partners (Pulles et al., 2014; Schiele, 2006). This is particularly important because the identification of startups requires a radically different approach. Startups are usually unknown partners without prior relations to the sourcing firm and therefore systematic search forms the basis for their identification. Hence, prior approaches to identify established external partners are not sufficient and were extended in this article by applying the concept of search breadth and depth to define successful search strategies for startups.

4.5.2. Managerial implications

Our findings show that broad and intensive search increases the success of search for startups. However, these findings do not allow to draw conclusions for managers on which search instruments are most powerful and effective. To do so, we analyzed the correlations of all single instruments on search success post-hoc (see Table 13). Findings show that the organization of pitch events has the highest positive impact on search success ($r = 0.462$, $p < 0.001$). Further, collaboration with venture capitalists and consulting firms, desk research, the investment in funds, and an open communication channel for startups are highly significant. Surprisingly, networks to universities do not show any significant effect on search success. Regarding the correlation of all search instruments with our second dependent variable, radical innovation capability, only networks with partners and non-partners show high significance. Thus, we conclude that networks are most important and the organization of own startup events provides highest direct search output. Overall, managers should invest in various search instruments, especially as some very effective ones do not imply high costs, e.g., an open innovation platform.

Table 13: Correlations of single identification instruments

Variable	Mean	SD	1	2	3	4	5	6	7	8	9	10	11	12	13
1 Desk research	3.16	1.43													
2 Scientific conferences/ publications	2.75	1.43	0.143												
3 Trade fairs/ exhibitions	2.90	1.25	0.359***	0.392***											
4 Self-organized pitch events	2.47	1.60	0.193+	0.211*	0.284**										
5 Fund of funds	1.93	1.69	0.347***	0.209*	0.401***	0.403***									
6 External scouting partner	2.08	1.65	0.096	0.216*	0.377***	0.233*	0.459***								
7 Scouting satellite	2.63	1.54	0.284**	0.137	0.244*	0.278**	0.394***	0.282**							
8 Networking with business partners	3.21	1.33	0.284**	0.307**	0.325**	0.355***	0.430***	0.472***	0.286**						
9 Network with universities/ research institutes	3.09	1.44	0.104	0.417***	0.225*	0.216*	0.115	0.243*	0.222*	0.170+					
10 Network with non-partnering firms	2.86	1.18	0.045	0.127	0.004	0.361***	0.094	0.086	0.165+	0.225*	0.260*				
11 E-mail, landing-, and web-page	2.13	1.58	0.309**	0.144	0.128	0.296**	0.348**	0.304**	0.128	0.150	0.242*	0.161			
12 Search success	3.23	0.79	0.425***	0.048	0.295**	0.462***	0.336**	0.392***	0.243*	0.379***	0.084	0.218*	0.397***		
13 Radical innovation capability	3.25	0.72	0.088	0.221*	0.193+	0.233*	0.204*	0.189+	0.071	0.279**	0.190+	0.302**	0.230*	0.371***	

$N = 97$.
+ $p < 0.1$, * $p < 0.05$, ** $p < 0.01$, *** $p < 0.001$.

4.5.3. Limitations and future research

This study has several limitations that should be respected for the interpretation of the results. First, our data set is relatively small. Taking into account that the investigated phenomenon is still in its infancy, the identification of managers that are systematically searching for startups was a challenging task. Second, this study includes subjective measures through the use of direct questions for respondents. Although we cannot exclude the presence of common method variance in the dataset, the design of the hypotheses, the application of ex ante remedies, and the statistical tests applied suggest that common method variance is not a cause for concern in our study. Third, our analyses facilitate a cross-sectional view of the firms in their current stage. Thus, our data renders testing for causal effects over time impossible, e.g., concerning the effect of successful search on firms' radical innovation capability. Still, we are able to show indications for the model and the dependencies. Longitudinal studies may help to test and substantiate some of our cross-sectional findings. In addition, we recommend to make use of objective data for future studies. Fourth, we did not consider how successful search results in radical product innovations. Our findings show that knowledge acquired due to search for startups increases firms' radical innovation capabilities. Still, we do not know the micro-processes behind the relations of successful search for startups, radical innovation capability and the actual generation of radically innovative products. Future studies could analyze these processes by applying qualitative designs. Further, while we focused on the identification phase, future research could focus on the post-identification stage, e.g., by investigating instruments that allow to evaluate the potential of identified startups before entering into collaborations. Finally, an interesting path for future research is the investigation of "dynamic managerial capabilities" (Helfat & Martin, 2015) with regard to corporate-startup relationships. Such studies could focus on the impact of search for startups on individual managers' cognitive learning. Overall, we hope that our research will stimulate organizational scholars to further examine startups as external stimuli for organizational learning.

Chapter 5 – Managing corporate-startup relationships: What matters for entrepreneurs?

Abstract:

Startups have become an important part of corporations' external technology sourcing portfolio. Nonetheless, startups may be reluctant to enter in a relationship with a corporation. Prior research on corporate-startup relationships has primarily focused on the benefits for corporations and neglected the perspective of startups. In a multiple case study, we analyze the collaborations of twelve startups to 30 different corporations to address this gap. The findings show that complementary assets, risks, as well as relational characteristics, influence the willingness of startups to enter such collaborations. We deduct nine propositions concerning, e.g., reputation and market access, misappropriation and the commitment of corporations. Further, our analysis highlights differences and similarities according to the maturity of startups. The study contributes to external technology sourcing literature and allows corporate managers to better understand the perspective of entrepreneurs in terms of engaging in strategic partnerships.

5.1. Introduction

Corporations need to access external technologies to enhance their innovativeness (Chesbrough, 2003; Laursen & Salter, 2006). The open innovation literature has identified various sources of external knowledge, such as suppliers, customers, universities, or competitors (Van de Vrande, 2013; West & Bogers, 2014). Suppliers as an external source have large impact on product innovation, but the knowledge corporate firms need to access cannot always be found within the existing networks of their organizations (Brusoni et al., 2001; Un et al., 2010). As a consequence, corporations have started to collaborate with startups even from distant industries (Gassmann et al., 2010; Weiblen & Chesbrough, 2015).

The literature on external technology sourcing has focused on the perspective of firms acquiring technology and thus neglected the perspective of providers (Monteiro et al., 2017; Rothaermel & Alexandre, 2009). Especially in the context of corporate-startup relationships, the startup perspective has not received sufficient attention (Katila et al., 2008). Prior findings show that corporations provide valuable complementary assets for startups in addition to funding (Park & Steensma, 2012). Startups can access various assets related to their technology, organization, or market access. Moreover, they face risks, such as misappropriation of IP and dependency (Diestre & Rajagopalan, 2012; Katila et al., 2008). Thus far, risks and complementary assets have rather been regarded as isolated. No prior study has addressed how entrepreneurs weight such factors when it comes to establishing their willingness to collaborate. Therefore, this article aims to address the following research question: *Which factors influence the willingness of startups to enter collaborations with corporations?*

Collaborative agreements can take various forms that differ in the commitment incurred, their reversibility, and their strategic goals (Van de Vrande, 2013; Van de Vrande et al., 2009). This study focuses on complementary assets and behavioral aspects of corporate-startup collaborations. Hence, we do not consider approaches that involve equity; rather, we focus on licensing, strategic buyer-supplier relationships as well as R&D collaborations as representatives of non-equity collaborations.

To answer the research question, we conduct an explorative case study among twelve startups that were partnering within the automotive industry (Miles & Huberman, 1994; Strauss & Corbin, 1998). The resulting propositions concern complementary assets, risks, and relational aspects linked to these collaborations. For all propositions, we distinguish startups by the maturity of their early-stage or market-ready technologies. Our study follows the rising interest in research on collaborations between small firms and large partners and especially on approaches to attract resources of a partner firm (Street & Cameron, 2007; Yang et al., 2014). The findings contribute to the literature on external technology sourcing and asymmetric partnerships. Managers of corporations benefit from this study since approaches of successful collaborations with startups are introduced.

The paper is organized in the following way. It starts with an analysis of existing literature on external technology sourcing and asymmetric partnerships between startups and corporations. The following paragraphs describe the framing of the study and data. Then, the results are shown by developing nine propositions that are discussed in detail. We end by discussing the implications of the research and further research directions.

5.2. Theoretical background

5.2.1. External technology sourcing

External technology sourcing has become an important part of firms' overall strategy (van Wijk et al., 2008; Wadhwa & Basu, 2013). To access these sources, prior research shows positive outcomes of approaches such as acquisitions (Ahuja & Katila, 2001), CVC investments (Dushnitsky & Lenox, 2006; Wadhwa et al., 2016), and strategic alliances (Lavie, 2007; Stuart, 2000). Further studies highlight the benefits of sourcing technologies from distant industries and new partners such as startups (Brunswicker & Hutschek, 2010; Gassmann et al., 2010).

Various external sources of technology are considered in literature, e.g., customers, suppliers, universities, or even competitors, which offer a promising way to extend the own knowledge base and increase the own firm's innovativeness (Felin & Zenger, 2014; Laursen & Salter, 2006). In addition, corporations recognize the potential of startups to rejuvenate their product portfolio (Weiblen & Chesbrough, 2015; Zaremba et al., 2016). In doing so, corporates hope to benefit from startups' unique entrepreneurial capabilities, such as alertness, creativity, flexibility, and willingness to take risks (Audretsch et al., 2014; Criscuolo et al., 2012; Marion et al., 2012).

Research on corporate-startup collaborations has focused on business venturing (Benson & Ziedonis, 2009; Narayanan, Yang, & Zahra, 2009). Further, non-equity collaborations such as buyer-supplier relationships, licensing, and strategic alliances have been applied (Hora & Dutta, 2013; Zaremba et al., 2016). As these approaches offer various advantages for startups, they are the focus of this study (Yang et al., 2014). In addition, program-based collaborations, such as accelerators (Pauwels et al., 2016) and incubators (Gerlach & Brem, 2015), have received growing attention.

5.2.2. Asymmetric partnerships between startups and corporations

Asymmetric partnerships have been discussed in literature, e.g., Minshall et al. (2008; 2010) and Prashantham and Birkinshaw (2008), showing that smaller firms run into specific problems when collaborating with corporations. From startups' perspective, accessing the right persons within large companies, identifying decision makers, lentil decisions, stagnate negotiations, and misunderstanding of their needs are major obstacles regarding such relations. With much more power in the collaboration, corporations can even endanger the survival of startups. But smaller firms also benefit from asymmetric partnerships as they can access new markets and technologies (H. Chen & Chen, 2002). Kalaignanam et al. (2007, p. 370) find that an asymmetric alliance is a "win-win or shareholder value-adding alliance for both the larger and smaller partner firms".

Benefits of asymmetric partnerships

Organizational capabilities are essential for firms to grow (Dosi et al., 2008; Penrose, 1959). In doing so, firms acquire new knowledge and synthesize existing knowledge (Kogut & Zander, 1992). Startups are well prepared to adapt their organizational routines by recombining, integrating, acquiring, or detaching resources (Eisenhardt & Martin, 2000; Sapienza, Autio, George, & Zahra, 2006; Zahra, Sapienza, & Davidsson, 2006). Nonetheless, startups face resource constraints when building their businesses, which can be compensated by accessing corporate partners (Stuart et al., 1999). Thereby, corporations considerably influence startups' innovation output (Garrido & Dushnitsky, 2016).

Technological capabilities are an important motivation to collaborate with other firms (Das & Teng, 2002; Harrison, Hitt, Hoskisson, & Ireland, 2001). Typically, startups possess certain specific knowledge, but they are often unable to advance their technology (Mitchell & Singh, 1992). In particular, they lack supplementary technological abilities to enrich and expand their innovation (Andersson & Xiao, 2016; Dahlstrand, 1997). Potential partners are especially attractive if they provide deep technological resources in order to benefit from their expertise (Ahuja, 2000). Further, young firms usually do not have sufficient manufacturing capabilities to scale products (Teece, 1986; Terjesen et al., 2011). Corporations can also provide such assets.

Another important complementary asset concerns organizational routines of startups (Zollo, Reuer, & Singh, 2002). In particular, recently established startups lack such capabilities

(Dushnitsky & Shapira, 2010). Therefore, mentoring by top management is an important asset offered by corporations. Mentoring is often part of specific programs to support startups. Examples are accelerators and incubators, which support startups at an early stage (Bergek & Norrman, 2008; Chesbrough & Brunswicker, 2014; Gerlach & Brem, 2015).

Moreover, startups often lack reputation and market access. Reputation and branding are key success factors for successful commercialization of innovations (Fombrun & Shanley, 1990). To avoid imitation or substitution from incumbents, firms have to reach a high degree of market penetration, with their new product or service (Ireland et al., 2003). However, as startups, they suffer from a liability of newness, and they often fail to bring their product successfully to market (Singh et al., 1986). Collaborating with partners possessing strong reputation increases startups' legitimacy. In this way, startups can build trust in their innovation and face fewer difficulties in convincing customers or other partners (Stuart, 2000; Stuart et al., 1999). Another way of developing legitimacy is by attracting venture capital, which also adds financial resources (Lee, Lee, & Pennings, 2001). In addition to enhancing the reputation of startups, corporations can become customers themselves and allow the startup to create a market for their product (Zaremba et al., 2016).

Challenges of asymmetric partnerships

First, dependency on the larger partner is a big issue for startups. A smaller partner may not even be able to take on its own business decisions once it has entered a collaboration (Street & Cameron, 2007). The underlying theoretical concept is resource dependence theory, which was introduced by Pfeffer and Salancik (1978). One basic proposition of this theory is that forming inter-organizational relationships helps organizations acquire resources that decrease interdependence and uncertainty. Unlike mergers, interdependencies are only partly absorbed if firms collaborate in alliances (Bouncken, 2015; Hillman, Withers, & Collins, 2009).

Second, misappropriation has most often been mentioned as a major obstacle to collaboration with a corporation from the perspective of startups (Brunswicker & Hutschek, 2010; Doz & Hamel, 1998). Startups even run the risk of becoming a victim of a collaboration with a corporation, as some fail to access organizational assets of corporations while providing their new technology (Alvarez & Barney, 2001). In addition, corporations may absorb the IP of the smaller partner (Deeds & Hill, 1996; Li, Eden, Hitt, & Ireland, 2008; Sulej, Stewart, & Keogh, 2001). The risk of misappropriation is especially high if the corporation has the ability to create value from the technology provided by the startup. An experienced R&D team might be a dangerous factor for a startup in this context (Diestre & Rajagopalan, 2012). In the worst case, a corporation will not consider a startup to be an equal partner, but may look for ways to take over a smaller firm (Doz, 1987). Thus, trust and collaborative objectives are necessary factors that shape these relationships (Inkpen & Currall, 2004).

5.3. Method

To address the research question, we applied an explorative, multiple case study (Flick, 2009; Silverman, 2016). This research design especially suits poorly understood phenomena (Strauss & Corbin, 1998; Yin, 2014). Further, this design allows us to identify common patterns and deduct general propositions (Miles & Huberman, 1994).

5.3.1. Framing the study

We regarded strategic buyer-supplier relationships, licensing, as well as R&D collaborations and program-based collaborations because this study focuses on complementary assets and relational aspects of corporate-startup collaborations. Hence, approaches that not primarily focus on knowledge transfer, e.g., corporate venturing, are excluded. Further, we differentiated startups according to their development stage. Technologies that are still under development or that have not passed the testing and validation phase are referred to as early-stage technologies. If the product is already available or just about to be launched, the technology can be referred to as market-ready (R. G. Cooper, 1990, 2008). Hence, we followed prior research in classifying the technology according to its development stage (R. G. Cooper, 1990), the growth stage of new ventures (Kazanjian, 1988) and the external sourcing continuum (Nambisan & Sawhney, 2007).

5.3.2. Data collection

Data were collected in collaboration with a large German OEM, which allowed us to contact selected startups of its portfolio. The OEM's portfolio contains more than 200 startups to which the OEM established closer relationships over the last three years. Startups within the portfolio were identified through various open innovation initiatives, e.g., startup pitch events, organized jointly by the OEM and external scouting partners. Within the OEM, cross-functional teams of R&D and purchasing managers are responsible for the open innovation initiatives. We selected those startups from the portfolio that were most knowledgeable about corporate-startup collaborations, based on the key informant approach (John & Reve, 1982). The automotive industry is particularly interesting to study. Owing to the very extensive specification, it is difficult for startups to obtain proof of concept. Therefore, corporations play an important role in supporting startups in this stage. Other reasons concern the industry's particular trend anticipation (Schiele, Horn, & Vos, 2011), specific danger of disruption (Blau, 2015) and the importance of external technology sources for OEMs (Wagner & Bode, 2011; Wynstra, Von Corswant, & Wetzels, 2010). Our choice of the automotive industry is in line with prior studies selecting this industry for investigations on open innovation (Homfeldt et al., 2017; Ili et al., 2010).

Following prior research on new firm creation, independent firms younger than eight years were included (McDougall et al., 1994). The sample contains both startups with established relations to corporations and startups without experiences concerning collaborations. The selected cases belong to different industries, e.g., ICT or manufacturing, and differ according to the development stage of their technology. Overall, we were able to report about 30 collaborations of twelve startups. Table 14 provides an overview of the cases.

The main sources of data were interviews that ranged from 30 minutes to 1.5 hours. In total, twelve semi-structured interviews were conducted by one of the authors. The questions were open to allow the respondents to answer in a broad way (for an overview see 9.3. Appendix Chapter 5). This approach helped to discover untouched areas. The interviewers put forward friendly and simple questions that also aimed to answer the more complex inquiries of this examination (Foddy, 1994; Yin, 2014). We allowed the interviewees to report in detail about their experiences with corporations. In addition, we discussed about potential future collaborations with corporations. In both cases, we asked for their motivation, benefits, drawbacks, and expectations regarding collaborations with corporations. Additionally, we investigated how they organized these relations.

To facilitate triangulation, multiple sources of data were used (Yin, 2014). Hence, interview data were enriched with publicly available materials of the startups, e.g., articles, Crunchbase, CB Insights, and company websites. Further, we accessed pitch decks and presentations directly from the startups, which allowed us to better understand the startups' products, partnerships, markets, funding and team structure. All existing data were gathered within our case study database in order to enforce reliability (Yin, 2014).

Table 14: Overview of cases

Startup	Founding year	Size	Funding	Country	Industry	Development stage	Existing collaboration	Types of collaborations	Job title of interview partner	Duration
Startup A	2010	10+	810k USD	Germany	ICT	Early-stage	No	2 R&D collaborations (1 rejected by the startup, 1 under discussion)	CEO	1 h
Startup B	2013	<10	none	Germany	Electronics	Early-stage	No	1 R&D collaboration (rejected by the corporate)	CEO	30 min
Startup C	2014	<10	200k USD	Germany	ICT	Early-stage	Yes	1 R&D collaboration, 1 incubator program, 1 accelerator program	Manager New Businesses	30 min
Startup D	2007	50+	16.2M USD	USA	ICT	Early-stage	Yes	1 R&D collaboration	Product Manager	1 h
Startup E	2013	10+	undisclosed	Germany	Manufacturing	Early-stage	Yes	2 R&D collaborations	CEO	1 h
Startup F	2014	<10	undisclosed	Germany	ICT	Market-ready	No	1 R&D collaborations (rejected by the startup)	Managing Director	30 min
Startup G	2011	<10	500k USD	Germany	ICT	Market-ready	Yes	3 R&D collaborations (1 rejected by the startup)	Managing Director	1.5 h
Startup H	2014	10+	200k USD	Switzerland	Logistics	Market-ready	Yes	4 Buyer-supplier relationships	CEO	30 min
Startup I	2014	10+	2M USD	Germany	Manufacturing	Market-ready	Yes	3 Licensing agreements (1 rejected by the startup)	Managing Director	45 min
Startup J	2008	10+	4.5M USD	USA	Energy	Market-ready	Yes	4 R&D collaborations	Senior Business Consultant	75 min
Startup K	2013	10+	1.5M USD	USA	Transportation	Market-ready	Yes	1 R&D collaboration, 2 buyer-supplier relationships	CEO	30 min
Startup L	2013	100+	38.9M USD	USA	ICT	Market-ready	Yes	3 buyer-supplier relationships	Director Sales	45 min

5.3.3. Data analysis

All interviews were transcribed and coded by the author who conducted the interviews shortly after completion. Hence, the data analysis was a continual process (Miles & Huberman, 1994). As there is existing literature on asymmetric partnerships and collaborations between startups and corporations, we made use of this knowledge. Therefore, the initial set of codes was extended during the analysis as more patterns evolved. We followed a multiple-step approach to cluster and analyze our data, as proposed by Gioia et al. (2013). Appendix Figure 8 shows the data structure differentiated into 1st order concepts, 2nd order concepts, and aggregated dimensions. To ensure reliability of the codes, we discussed the deducted codes and aggregated dimensions with industry experts, entrepreneurs, and academic scholars. As the review with experts showed that all codes were meaningful and important, none of the codes was dropped.

5.4. Results

The willingness of startups to collaborate with corporations differs in some aspects depending on the development stage of their technology. The analysis regards complementary assets offered by corporations and underlying risks of these collaborations. Finally, relational aspects are discussed. While the maturity of startups' technologies influences their willingness to enter collaborations with corporations, we did not identify any differences depending on prior experiences with corporations.

First, compared with startups possessing market-ready technologies, early-stage startups face the problem that they do not know whether their innovation fits market needs and whether their business is suitable to survive on the market. By gaining a corporation partner, they have the chance to receive sound feedback on their technology and business approach. Moreover, corporations may provide technological resources, such as specific laboratories or test centers. One of the interviewees stated that they would have had to pay high fees to obtain specific test results that their corporate partner provided them for free (Startup E). Further, corporations may help to improve startups' technology in order to reach market readiness. Consequently, the first proposition can be formulated as follows:

Proposition 1a: *Technological resources provided by corporations have a stronger positive effect on the willingness to collaborate for startups with early-stage technologies compared with startups possessing market-ready technologies.*

As startups are not known on the market and as they often have not started to expand the commercialization of their product, accessing a corporation as a customer is a major advantage. First, corporations are seen as good customers that one interviewee stated as follows: "In the end, they [corporations] are good customers which actually pay in the end." (Startup E) The analyzed startups followed different approaches, such as licensing or selling their final product, or even starting to first sell a minimal viable product. Direct commercialization is only one aspect. Collaborations with corporations also increase the reputation of startups as the corporation becomes a reference customer. One founder stated: "(…) [due to the collaboration with a corporation] we receive a lot of visibility, so it is good for the customers and venture capitalists." (Startup C) Another entrepreneur described how his firm takes advantage of the reputation of their collaboration partner: "The marketing effect, when we write about this [the collaboration] on our homepage is a good thing for us." (Startup E) Another aspect is the sales channel of the corporate, which can be accessed. But reputation does not only help to access other customers and funding but also to become a more attractive employer. Established collaborations with prestigious corporations may attract additional qualified labor. Overall, a second proposition regarding provided resources by corporations can be introduced that applies to any startup:

Proposition 1b: *Reputation of and market access provided by corporations increase the willingness of startups with early-stage technologies and market-ready technologies to collaborate.*

Some collaborative agreements between corporations and startups include organizational support for newly founded startups, e.g., mentoring by corporate managers. Especially, programs like accelerators and incubators explicitly provide mentoring, which was mentioned by the founder of Startup C. Thereby, mentors can also be serial entrepreneurs or business angels (Pauwels et al., 2016). Less formal organizational support was also reported by other startups. Corporations can thereby open doors and support by, e.g., highlighting ways for the startup to ship their product to the USA (Startup F). As these points were only mentioned by startups with early-stage technologies, the third proposition concerning provided resources can be stated in the following way:

Proposition 1c: *Organizational support has a stronger positive impact on the willingness to collaborate with corporations for startups with early-stage compared to startups with market-ready technologies.*

After evaluating the effect of resources provided by corporations, the following propositions show the "dark side"—the risks—of collaborations. First, especially early-stage startups run the risk that their technology is misappropriated. The interviewee of Startup A was reporting about a very open approach of misappropriation. A corporation tried to buy a majority share of this startup merely to squeeze it out of the market. To avoid this scenario, one startup decided to follow another strategy: "Therefore, if we start collaborations with bigger firms— we actually have one—then these are complementary firms, in this sense that their core competence is not the same as ours. But they contribute something that is helpful or they contribute something that complements the products." (Startup E) Another founder reported that they were offered an exit in a very early phase, which was rejected as they wanted to first benefit from their patents themselves (Startup B). The first proposition regarding risks has different implications for startups depending on the development stage of the technology and can be stated as follows:

Proposition 2a: *The risks of misappropriation have a negative impact on the willingness of startups to collaborate with corporations and affect startups with early-stage technologies stronger than startups with market-ready technologies.*

Becoming dependent of corporations is another fear of startups. Dependency can affect startups in different dimensions such as product development or sales. One interviewee referred to their ideation and development phase and stated: "We are looking for collaboration partners who allow us to work independently—just because I go together with a big one does not mean that our creativity or jester's license gets decreased" (Startup A). Further, startups may become dependent regarding their sales activities as well. One founder stated that they would run the risk of "entering a state of dependency concerning the market access" (Startup F). Discussing their personal background, all founders were convinced of their decision to become an entrepreneur, especially because of the independence coming along with this career. Consequently, the following proposition can be reported:

Proposition 2b:　　　　*Startups' motivation to collaborate with corporations decreases if they run the risk of dependency independent of the development stage of their technology.*

Further discussions showed that the factor reputation and market access is the most important one for startups. This factor is followed by exclusion of the risks dependency and misappropriation. Less important are the factors technological resources and organizational support.

In addition to the benefits and risks, the results of the interviews clearly highlight different aspects concerning the collaborative behavior that applies to all startups independent of their development stage. First, our results further show that startups with market-ready technologies prefer looser collaborative agreements, e.g., buyer-supplier relationships or licensing, with corporations. In contrast, startups at an early-stage rather look for closer collaborations in the form of joint R&D projects. Other approaches for closer collaborations are corporate programs, such as accelerators and incubators. As illustrated in Table 14, only firms with market-ready technologies entered looser collaboration. In addition, some of the more mature startups, such as Startup K, also formed R&D collaborations. Considering these differences, the following proposition can be formulated:

Proposition 3a:　　　　*Startups with market-ready technologies prefer looser collaborative agreements with corporations than startups with early-stage technologies that look for closer collaborations.*

Almost all participants stated that they were not happy with the speed of the collaboration which concerns both, the pre-collaboration and collaboration phase. One of the founders described their experience prior to the collaboration in the following way: "They [corporations] reach out to us and request a lot of information and also want to receive an offer quickly and then everything takes incredibly long. Then it takes three to four weeks until we receive sampling parts, then these need to pass security checks and several tests are conducted (…), and finally the statement reaches us that they are willing to acquire a facility, and then it is said that it is in the budget for next year, and finally procurement reaches out, and then until you get a supplier number (…)." (Startup E) Once the collaboration is set up, things still simply take too long in the corporate world, as another entrepreneur stated: "[The corporation] had to first learn how to act with startups and technology licensing since the old concept was only compatible for the collaboration with big firms. Here, the contract negotiations lasted more than half a year due to a manager without experience regarding startups (…)." (Startup I) The demand for higher speed can be summarized in the next proposition:

Proposition 3b: *Higher speed in the collaboration increases startups' willingness to collaborate with a corporation independent of the development stage of their technology.*

The pure size of corporations makes it hard for startups to identify the most suitable contact person for their topic within the organization. The interview partner of Startup D explained their confusion: "To put it more generally, the organizational structure is really complex. And sometimes for a startup, it is really hard to figure out who we need to be talking to." Some interviewed founders argued that they would have appreciated to speak directly to C-level executives in order to address their topic. One founder brought the problem to a point: "(…) as a small company working with a larger organization, you are generally working in the middle management areas and these positions can change. And so what is a human being that is moved into a different position and a new guy coming in that decides to go on different routes (…)." (Startup J) Another point that has been brought up is that startups prefer to address the core organization of a corporation not its sister company or associated enterprise. Consequently, the third proposition concerning collaborative behavior can be formulated:

Proposition 3c: *Accessing the right contact persons increases startups' willingness to collaborate with a corporation independent of the development stage of their technology.*

Finally, it is very important for startups to form strategic partnerships with corporations. Describing this strategic partnership, a multi-dimensional approach has to be followed to address the following aspects: trust, scope and the development of the relationship. First, trust is a result of strategic partnerships, and it also helps to improve collaborations. The representative of Startup D reported that they started working on a project without having a purchase order. Further, the scope of the project influences the trust of startups. If they can rely on holistic projects, they can more efficiently manage their resources (Startup D). In addition, developing the relationship over time motivates startups to collaborate with corporations, as one of the interviewed founders stated: "(…) [we start with] a display of how it works and then we move to the small test installation where we can show that the technology can work with the customer (…) and then we would move into the building a larger field pilot (…)." (Startup J) Thus, startups look for commitment, as one of the founders stated: "Because they are such a large business and this is a new product line for them that comes along with that collaboration, it is not essential for them yet (…). They can say [that] they are purely decided to move in this direction, but I can only assume that a company as big [as theirs] is seeing this more as let's put our feet in the water and let's see where this takes us. And since they have so many other product lines and sources of revenue, it is not unbelievable to think that this does not work out in the short term (…). They can pull out as they have so many other industries they are working on. Whereas us, we are all in on this, this is our business. We have one product, essentially, that is the direction we are moving in. We have a long-term gain plan of how we calculate this market and where we want to go. At this point we are past the point where we are just seeing this as a test of where we may just pull back and go to a different product." (Startup K) Consequently, the last proposition can be summarized as follows:

Proposition 3d: *Establishing strategic partnerships enhances the motivation of startups to collaborate with corporations independent of the development stage of their technology.*

To sum up the findings, startups' willingness to collaborate with corporate organizations depends on provided resources, expected risks and the collaborative behavior of corporations. Figure 6 summaries all identified factors and illustrates the distinction of the applicability of the findings according to the development stage of startups' technologies.

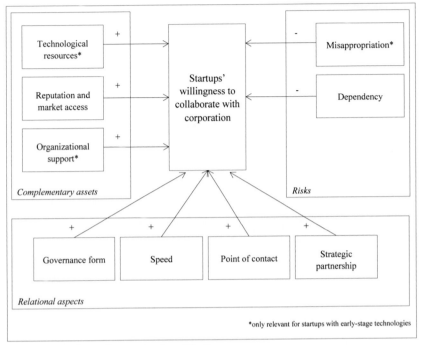

Figure 6: Overview and categorization of findings

5.5. Discussion

This study examines (1) complementary assets, (2) risks, and (3) relational aspects concerning collaborations between startups and corporations taking the perspective of startups. In the following, we discuss our findings under the light of literature on external technology sourcing and asymmetric partnerships.

First, startups, independent of their development stage, search for reputation and market access when collaborating with corporations. In doing so, startups enhance their legitimacy (Stuart, 2000; Stuart et al., 1999). Other factors differ according to the development stage of their technology. One of these factors concerns technological resources. As startups with market-ready technologies have managed to access or build resources to scale and enhance their technologies, early-stage startups may still be confronted with hurdles concerning this phase (Andersson & Xiao, 2016). Hence, powerful and well-established R&D organizations are important assets that startups want to access. Moreover, startups with more experienced founders and more mature technologies show less openness or needs for organizational support in the form of mentoring. Mentoring as a complementary asset is mainly discussed in literature on corporate incubation (Bergek & Norrman, 2008; Pauwels et al., 2016). As corporate incubation programs target early-stage startups, our findings are in line with this stream of research as in our sample entrepreneurs in more mature startups did not ask for organizational support.

Second, our results highlight risks for startups accompanying collaborations with corporations, such as becoming dependent of the more powerful partner. In general, entrepreneurs try to avoid the tight boarders of corporate organizations. This finding is not surprising as autonomy is closely linked to entrepreneurial orientation. Autonomy describes "the ability and will to be self-directed in the pursuit of opportunities" (Lumpkin & Dess, 1996, p. 140). Another risk is misappropriation. Startups in earlier stages run higher risks, as they rather create new knowledge together with corporations following a co-exploration approach (Parmigiani & Rivera-Santos, 2011). On the one hand, they have not arrived at establishing powerful protection mechanisms, such as patents (Deeds & Hill, 1996; Li et al., 2008; Sulej et al., 2001). On the other hand, they miss absorptive capacity to benefit from organizational assets provided by corporations (Alvarez & Barney, 2001; Cohen & Levinthal, 1990). Thus, close collaboration with corporations is not always beneficial in early phases.

Third, we identify several relational aspects that matter for startups. Our findings show that the more mature the technology of a startup, the looser the collaborative agreement is designed. Startups with early-stage technologies can benefit from closer collaborations as they can grow their knowledge base by combing existing knowledge with knowledge provided by partnering corporations (Fjeldstad, Snow, Miles, & Lettl, 2012; Un et al., 2010). In contrast, startups with market-ready technologies benefit more from pecuniary compensations through, e.g., IP licensing (Chesbrough & Brunswicker, 2014). Thus, we follow existing governance literature in the entrepreneurial field showing the influence of the technological maturity on the proximity of the relation (Van de Vrande et al., 2009; Yang et al., 2014). The further analysis shows that the speed of collaborations matters for startups. One aspect is that founders do not align with more languorous processes of corporations. Also bringing the first product to market is crucial for startups in order to achieve visibility, gain financial independence through early cash flows and increase actuarial survival rate (Schoonhoven et al., 1990). Thus, startups benefit from higher speed in the collaboration with corporations if these collaborations serve their product ideas. In order to initiate and conduct collaborations, startups depend on the assigned contacts to the corporate. If the assigned mangers underperform and do not recognize the importance of working with the startups, collaborations may fail (De Meyer, 1999). Prior research has further shown that collaboration partners benefit from prior personal relations to the contact persons within a firm (Larson, 1992). Benefits of strategic partnerships are bilateral. The results are in line with existing studies highlighting the importance of attributes like commitment, coordination and trust (Gassmann et al., 2010; Mohr & Spekman, 1994).

5.5.1. Theoretical contributions

Our findings contribute to theory in several ways. To start with, we add to literature on external technology sourcing since we focus on startups as one source of external technology and knowledge. In addition, we illuminate the prospect of the firm providing the technology which has been underrepresented in prior studies (Monteiro et al., 2017; Rothaermel & Alexandre, 2009). Since this study regards collaborative approaches that exclude equity, we follow previous discussions on leaner approaches of collaborations between startups and corporations (Andersson & Xiao, 2016; Weiblen & Chesbrough, 2015). By showing that startups can access important complementary assets by collaborating with corporations, our findings add to prior research on resource attraction in the context of small firms and large partners (Street & Cameron, 2007; Yang et al., 2014).

Moreover, our research advances literature on asymmetric partnerships. On the one hand, we highlight organizational capabilities that can be provided to support the smaller partner (Katila et al., 2008; Kogut & Zander, 1992). On the other hand, findings address dependencies for small firms when entering collaborations with corporations. These are in line with prior findings (Alvarez & Barney, 2001). We extend the work of Minshall et al. (2008; 2010) by differentiating startups according to the development stage of their technology as well as by providing additional factors which matter for asymmetric partnerships between startups and corporations, e.g., the commitment of corporates to form strategic partnerships. The formulation of nine propositions allows us to create a framework addressing this specific type of asymmetric partnerships from the startup's perspective (see Figure 6).

Finally, our findings highlight paths to increase the attractiveness of corporations as partners for startups in a similar way as the preferred customer concept (Schiele, Veldman, et al., 2011). Becoming preferred customer has become increasingly important in buyer-supplier relationships as few highly innovative suppliers are courted by many competitors (Schiele, 2012). Examples can be found within the automotive (Wagner & Bode, 2011), biotech (Powell et al., 1996), or software industry (Lavie, 2007). Overall, the attractiveness of corporations as partners for startups decides about the success of their external technology sourcing initiatives.

5.5.2. Managerial contributions

Digitalization affects all industries, even product-focused industries such as the automotive industry (Svahn et al., 2017). Therefore, managers have to anticipate new technologies and business models which are accompanied by technology and digital entrepreneurship as well as sharing economy (Giones & Brem, 2017; Nambisan, 2017; Richter et al., 2017). Examples can be found among the studied firms, e.g., Startup D offers approaches to commercialize car data and thereby enables OEMs to create new revenue models. But developments caused by the sharing economy can also evolve to a threat for corporations. As reported in the study of Richter et al. (2017), new trends in car sharing may limit the need to own cars and consequently reduce the demand for new vehicles.

Our results show how managers can enhance the willingness of startups to partner with corporations in order to benefit from their technologies. Thereby, some aspects are inherent to corporate organizations in general. Any collaboration with a corporation offers the chance to access a market, build reputation or validate the technology. Further, startups may always run the risk of dependency or misappropriation when partnering with a corporation. Hence, these factors do not offer much potential for corporations to differentiate in their competition for the most attractive startups. Instead, the attractiveness of a corporation partner is most influenced by relational aspects. One aspect is the selected governance form. If the technology of startups is in an earlier stage, joint R&D projects should be offered. For startups with more mature technologies, entering a buyer-supplier relationship and becoming a customer, adds the highest value for startups. Further, managers can ensure that startups talk with the right people within their organization, speed up discussions internally and establish strategic relationships. Overall, we recommend that managers install quick track programs for startups. Such programs should include leaner processes which allow to handle the collaboration with higher speed and increased awareness of the management.

5.5.3. Limitations and future research

Our study is not without limitations. Although the study was conducted within the automotive context, the startups originate various environments. Hence, there are external conditions and dynamics that were not considered. Katila and Shane (2005) focus on four innovation-related factors that illustrate the interrelationship of external market factors and organizational attributes: competition on the market, market size, accessibility of capital, and manufacturing intensity. For a more holistic perspective, these environmental factors may be respected for future research.

Our analysis focuses on firm-level factors and does not consider individuals' decisions regarding partnerships with corporations. Fauchart and Gruber (2011) differentiate three types of founder identities which differ according to the basic social motivation, basis of self-evaluation, and the frame of reference. While darwinians focus on themselves and their business, communitarians are driven by advancing their community. The third group are missionaries which target the goals of society and are estimated to be the rarest in many industries. Future research could analyze how entrepreneurs' social identity shapes key decisions regarding business development and their relationships with corporations.

Further, the propositions only build on a small sample of twelve cases within one industry. Thus, the generalizability of the propositions is limited and will have to be tested in a larger scaled study. Any quantitative approach would enhance these findings. Still, we want to show one specific direction, further research may go. Conjoint approaches in the form of discrete choice experiments have recently been applied in entrepreneurship and innovation literature (Fischer & Henkel, 2013; Hoenig & Henkel, 2015). Applying this method to the partner selection of startups would advance entrepreneurship literature. Further, research methodology in this respective field would be enriched.

Future research could also focus on collaboration networks among startups and their impact on corporate-startup relationships. Complementary collaborations among startups offer various advantages, e.g., less cultural barriers and joint-target formulation. One of the founders put it in the following way: "We refer each other companies, we have a similar customer base, and we think alike in a lot of ways and so it makes it an easy collaboration." (Startup K)

5.6. Conclusions

To conclude, this multiple case study discusses factors that influence the willingness of startups to collaborate with corporations. For startups complementary assets, risks and the way corporations form the relationship matter. The deducted propositions are set into perspective according to the development stage of startups. Our study shows similarities and differences for startups with technologies in an early stage compared to startups with market-ready technologies. Nonetheless, many developed propositions apply to both types of startups. The findings contribute to literature on external technology sourcing and asymmetric partnerships. As the findings build on qualitative data, we show interesting future research paths borrowing methods from other fields. Finally, managers of corporations may use our findings to rethink their approaches to collaborate with startups.

Chapter 6 – Discussion

This dissertation analyzes how corporations access knowledge provided by startups and highlights the implications on the searching organization. Chapter 6 reflects on the key findings of the preceding chapters by discussion the findings and implications under the light of the proposed research questions. Moreover, the implications for the literature and practice as well as directions for future research are discussed.

6.1. Main findings

This dissertation investigates the primary research question *"which approaches do corporations follow to access knowledge provided by startups and what are the implications on the organization?"*. This question focuses on *how* corporations identify startups and *why* they follow the path of corporate-startup collaborations. In the following, the main findings are highlighted and reflected on.

First, we introduce search approaches for the identification of startups. Structured search approaches are particularly important since the identification of startups requires a radically different approach compared to identifying established suppliers (Pulles et al., 2014; Schiele, 2006). As startups are usually unknown partners without prior relations to the sourcing firm, the introduction of structured search represents the basis for their identification. Hence, existing approaches to identify established suppliers are not directly applicable to the identification of startups. Chapter 3 highlights overall eleven search instruments, a structured identification process and four organizational approaches to identify startups. In chapter 4 we find that searching broadly and intensively increases the search success (i.e., the identification of adequate and value creating startups). Finally, chapter 5 shows how corporations may act to become an attractive partner for startups by analyzing how complementary assets, risks, and relational characteristics influence the willingness of startups to enter collaborations with corporations. We conclude that startups still have problems dealing with languorous processes of corporations and accessing the right contact persons. In addition, startups miss commitment of partnering corporations.

Second, our findings underline that corporations should engage in the search for startups. In chapter 2 we find empirical support that startups provide ideas with higher novelty and customer benefit. Although ideas provided by startups experience several constraints regarding the implementation for corporate organizations, the results underline the importance of following this path. Moreover, chapter 4 highlights that already the search for startups has positive implications on the organizational capabilities of the searching firm. By continuously screening startup ideas and interacting with entrepreneurial teams, firms expand their radical innovation capabilities. Consequently, we provide evidence that the generation of new knowledge is supported by interactions with new partners without prior business relations (Lavie & Rosenkopf, 2006; Stettner & Lavie, 2014) and by including distant knowledge (Katila & Ahuja, 2002).

To sum it up, this dissertation provides insights how corporations can access knowledge from startups by introducing structured search approaches and establishing relationships based on equality. As a consequence, corporate organizations benefit from truly innovative ideas and are able to enhance their radical innovation capabilities. Overall, the findings underline the importance of investing time and resources in the pre-collaboration phase to be able to access knowledge provided by startups.

6.2. Findings and theoretical contributions per chapter

The following paragraphs provide answers to the proposed research questions and highlight the theoretical implications, which have been investigated in chapters 2 to 5:

- Chapter 2 – *How do startups and established suppliers perform compared to each other in generating promising innovation ideas?*
- Chapter 3 – *Which approaches do corporations apply to search for startups?*
- Chapter 4 – *How do corporations achieve successful search for startups to enhance their organizational capabilities?*
- Chapter 5 – *Which factors influence the willingness of startups to enter collaborations with corporations?*

Based on a comparison of 314 supplier and startup ideas, *chapter 2* provides empirical evidence that ideas generated by startups are characterized by a higher degree of novelty and customer benefit compared to ideas originating established suppliers. On the downside, the results illustrate that startup ideas are less likely to be implemented, which implies that supplier ideas fit better in with existing technologies and create more valuable business opportunities while meeting technical and economic criteria. However, the startup ideas that were decided to be implemented possessed higher degree of novelty.

From a theoretical perspective, this study contributes to external knowledge sourcing literature by providing evidence that drawing on knowledge from more distant domains (e.g., Katila & Ahuja, 2002; Rosenkopf & Almeida, 2003), that is, from beyond the established supply base, facilitates the identification of promising solutions. Moreover, this chapter follows the call for research on startups' innovative capabilities in the early stages of a firm's innovation process (Kickul et al., 2011). Further, we contribute to the creation of a more holistic view on the value of the diverse set of external sources of ideas. While the existing research has solely focused on comparing the quality of ideas generated by different user types (Poetz & Schreier,

2012; Schweisfurth, 2017), this study is the first to consider suppliers and startups as increasingly important external sources of ideas.

Chapter 3 analyzes organizational structures and the implementation of search for startups within corporate organizations. First, we identify four approaches to organize the search for startups that differ regarding the involvement of internal stakeholders and their closeness to the ordinary organization. Among them, we identify two internal approaches that are not limited due to missing cross-organizational (Rosenkopf & Nerkar, 2001) and intra-organizational (Ancona & Caldwell, 1992) linkages. In addition, a detailed identification process model is illustrated as well as seven pull and four push instruments (such as startup pitch events or networks) to realize the search for startups.

This part of the dissertation contributes to external knowledge sourcing by highlighting how organizations can identify external partners beyond their established networks and provide a necessary extension to prior research limited to the identification of innovation partners within established networks (Pulles et al., 2014; Schiele, 2006). The collected data allows to distinguish different organizational structures that are installed by corporations to realize boundary spanning to access knowledge provided by startups (Rosenkopf & Almeida, 2003; Rosenkopf & Nerkar, 2001). Thereby, we extend prior research that has exclusively studied external scouting units embedded in local startup environments (Doz et al., 2001; Gassmann & Gaso, 2004; Monteiro & Birkinshaw, 2017). Finally, our findings indicate how procurement departments contribute to the search for startups and thus support prior findings emphasizing the important role of procurement in the innovation process of corporate organization (Schoenherr & Wagner, 2016; Wagner, 2012).

Chapter 4 highlights positive effects of broad and intensive search for startups. In addition, the findings illustrate the subsequent benefits for the searching firms' radical innovation capability. More specifically, we show that search breadth and search depth have positive impact on search success (i.e., the identification of adequate and value creating startups) and that the effects of these search activities on the searching firms' radical innovation capability (i.e., the ability to generate innovations that significantly transform existing solutions) are positive as well. In contrast to prior studies investigating the outcome of search, our study finds linear relationships as over-searching is not an issue in this context, which would imply curvilinear effects (Rothaermel & Alexandre, 2009; Wadhwa et al., 2016). In line with similar study designs, the results show that search depth is much less common than search breadth (J. Chen et al., 2011; Chiang & Hung, 2010; Laursen & Salter, 2006). Finally, we confirm our proposition that the successful search for startups is accompanied by impulses to generate radical innovations and subsequently expand the firms' organizational capabilities (Colombo et al., 2017; Zollo & Winter, 2002).

The contribution to external knowledge sourcing literature concerns on the one hand the transfer of frequently applied measures for search strategies to the context of the search for startups (Katila & Ahuja, 2002; Laursen & Salter, 2006). On the other hand, we show that knowledge originating startups provides additional new variations of knowledge and explorative ideas to solve existing problems (Katila & Ahuja, 2002; March, 1991). In extension to prior research, our findings underline that already the search for startups provides stimuli for the searching organizations to generate radical innovations. Hence, our findings illustrate that firms start building own explorative learning capabilities as a consequence of constantly dealing with external radical innovations provided by startups. In particular, we highlight the leading role of interacting with new partners without prior business relations to facilitate explorative learning (Levinthal & March, 1993; March, 1991; Stettner & Lavie, 2014).

The findings of *chapter 5* show that complementary assets, risks as well as relational characteristics influence the willingness of startups to enter collaborations with corporations. We deduct nine propositions concerning, e.g., reputation and market access, misappropriation and the commitment of corporations, and differentiate startups according to the maturity of their technology in market-ready and early-stage. Benefits of strategic partnerships are bilateral. Our results are in line with existing studies highlighting the importance of attributes like commitment, coordination and trust (Gassmann et al., 2010; Mohr & Spekman, 1994).

This chapter illuminates the prospect of the knowledge providing firm and thus we add to an underrepresented perspective of external knowledge sourcing literature (Monteiro et al., 2017; Rothaermel & Alexandre, 2009). We extend the work of Minshall et al. (2008; 2010) as we differentiate startups according to the development stage of their technology. In addition, relational factors are added to literature such as the commitment of corporations to engage in strategic partners. Moreover, we illustrate how corporations can become attractive partners for startups, comparable to the preferred customer principle originating buyer-supplier relationships (Pulles et al., 2016; Schiele, 2012). Overall, the attractiveness of corporations as partners for startups decides about the success of their attempts to access knowledge provided by startups.

6.3. Managerial implications

This dissertation also bears straightforward implications for managers and practitioners. By showing how managers can access knowledge provided by startups, we highlight ways to respond to the challenges (such as missing expertise and knowledge) of the digital revolution (Nambisan, 2017; Svahn et al., 2017).

We suggest that firms should reach beyond their established supply base and integrate startups in the ideation phase of their innovation process. Yet, startups can and should not replace established suppliers. Depending on their innovation strategy, firms should consider suppliers as well as startups. While startup ideas provide by far higher radical innovation potential (i.e., high novelty combined with high customer benefit of the idea), ideas provided by established supplier have the potential to incrementally improve existing solutions and allow to gain quick wins. Thus, we recommend to include both, startups and established suppliers, in the innovation process to generate a successful innovation portfolio.

In addition, this dissertation provides insights how corporations can identify startups from an organizational perspective. The introduced structural approaches and instruments differ in their cost of implementation, which should be considered before taking decisions. Further, our findings highlight that broad and intensive search increases the success of search for startups. The correlation analysis of all search instruments with search success provides evidence that the organization of pitch events has the highest positive impact on search success. As the collaboration with venture capitalists and consulting firms, desk research, the investment in funds, and an open communication channel for startups are highly significant as well, we conclude that managers should invest in various search instruments to identify adequate and value creating startups. In order to access knowledge from startups, corporations also need to become attractive partners for startups. Concerning relational aspects, managers can ensure that startups talk to the right people within their organization, speed up discussions internally and establish strategic relationships. As corporations will find it difficult to interact with startups following standard processes, we recommends to install "quick track programs" for startups, which include leaner processes.

Overall, the present dissertation provides an overview of factors that corporations have to fulfil to become attractive partners for startups and to achieve preferred customer status (Schiele, Calvi, & Gibbert, 2012; Steinle & Schiele, 2008). Table 15 summarizes basic and differentiating factors. In order to access knowledge provided by startups, corporations need to establish appropriate organizational structures. Hence, the introduction of structured processes and application of different search instruments form the basis to tap into startup innovation. As every corporation possesses specific technological expertise in their respective field and may provide a market for startups, corporations cannot differentiate along these factors. In contrary, reputation, funding and mentoring allow differentiation since the strength of brands differs as well as the design of investments and mentoring programs. Moreover, the way corporations interact with startups may decide about startups' willingness to collaborate. To conclude, we provide an overview of factors that decide about the success of establishing corporate-startup relationships.

Table 15: Basic and differentiating factors

Basic factors	Differentiating factors
▪ Market access	▪ Reputation
▪ Technological feedback	▪ Funding
▪ Organizational factors	▪ Mentoring
○ Organizational structures	○ Organizational training
○ Identification processes	○ Technological training
○ Set of identification instruments	▪ Relational characteristics
	○ Independency for startups
	○ Avoidance of misappropriation
	○ Adequate collaboration approaches
	○ Fast decisions
	○ Single point of contact
	○ Top management attention
	○ Commitment to relation

6.4. Future research

Considering the findings and limitations of this dissertation, interesting path for future research can be deducted. We identified interesting paths on the firm and individual level that may advance research on external knowledge sourcing.

First, existing research has not regarded what exactly motivates startups to take part in the early stages of corporations' NPD processes and to provide ideas of high quality. This applies as well for more established supplying firms (LaBahn & Krapfel, 2000). In chapter 2, we find that suppliers and startups were equally motivated by the fact to advance business relations with the automotive OEM. Yet, future research may focus on more diverse motivational factors, such as incentives or relational aspects.

Second, the literature misses an analysis of how to make corporate-startup relations work and thus how to advance beyond the pre-collaboration phase in order to implement startup ideas to products. Qualitative longitudinal studies covering the process from identification to collaboration should be used to better understand why collaborations fail and how collaborations work successfully, thus providing helpful guidance to practitioners.

As a third path for future research, scholars may analyze different approaches to govern corporate-startup relationships. Van de Vrande (2013) highlights the importance of a broader array of governance modes for external knowledge sourcing beyond strategic alliances. To address specific needs of startups, Weiblen and Chesbrough (2015) introduce lean approaches for corporate-startup collaborations. As an extension, future research may investigate which approaches imply the highest benefit for both, startups and corporations. Building on literature on governance modes (e.g., Gulati & Singh, 1998; Santoro & McGill, 2005; Van de Vrande et al., 2009; Villalonga & McGahan, 2005), Figure 7 provides an overview of collaboration approaches for corporate-startup relationships. The portfolio differentiates along a continuum of arms-length transactions and fully integrated solutions. Corporate-startup collaborations can either be loosely or closely coupled and may include equity. Each approach offers a specific set of assets for startups, such as funding, market access, or technological support. Depending on the specific needs of startups, corporations should consider different collaboration approaches to become an attractive partner. While sourcing and licensing primarily imply market access for startups, the main asset of corporate venturing is funding. Joint R&D projects allow startups to participate in specific technological assets of the corporate partner. Startup programs, such as incubators or accelerators, provide a broad spectrum of assets including mentoring and funding. Independent of the governance choice, startups benefit from the reputation of the partnering corporation. Future research may analyze the implications of governance choices for relationships with startups. Especially, the perspective of startups may be considered when choosing the appropriate governance approach.

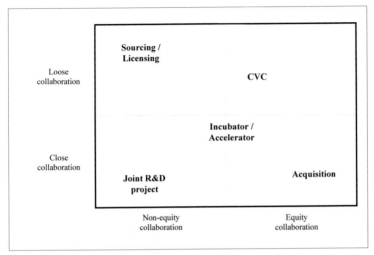

Figure 7: Corporate-startup collaboration portfolio

Fourth, an interesting path for future research may be the investigation of "dynamic managerial capabilities" (Helfat & Martin, 2015) with regard to corporate-startup relationships. In particular, the implications on managers' cognitive learning could be investigated that is caused by dealing with startups, e.g., due to identifying startups, evaluating their technologies and ideas, and collaborating with entrepreneurs. Thus, further research on the implications of stimuli provided by startups may advance the research on individual learning.

Finally, entrepreneurs' social identity may be considered in the pre-collaboration phase of corporate-startup relationships. Fauchart and Gruber (2011) identify three types of identities that can be differentiated according to the basic social motivation, basis of self-evaluation and the frame of reference. While darwinians focus on themselves and their business, communitarians are driven by advancing their community. The third group are missionaries that target the goals of society, and are estimated to be the rarest in many industries. Future research may regard how entrepreneurs' social identity shapes key decisions regarding business development and their relationships with corporations. From a methodological perspective, discrete choice experiments may serve as the most promising approach to investigate this question. Especially, as conjoint research has been recently been applied in entrepreneurship and innovation research (Fischer & Henkel, 2013; Hoenig & Henkel, 2015).

7. Academic output per chapter

This dissertation is cumulative in nature and is based on four individual papers (chapter 2 to 5). The following list summarizes the included publications.

Chapter 2. Homfeldt, F., Simon, F., Rese, A., 2018. Suppliers versus startups: Where do better innovation ideas come from?

This paper is to be resubmitted to Research Policy. A prior versions was presented at the Autouni Research Colloquium, Wolfsburg, Germany, 2017.

Chapter 3. Simon, F., Delke, V. F., Schiele, H., Harms, R., 2018. Identifying partners outside existing networks: How do corporate organizations search for startups?

This paper is to be resubmitted to an international journal. A prior version was presented at the 27th IPSERA conference in Athens, Greece, March 2018.

This paper was also presented at the Autouni Research Colloquium, Wolfsburg, Germany, 2016 and has been published in a German version for practitioners as Simon, F., Delke, V. F., 2017. Start-ups als Innovations-Partner: Eine Analyse komplexer Suchprozesse in der Automobilindustrie. Supply Chain Management, 1, 23-27.

Chapter 4. Simon, F., Homfeldt, F., Schiele, H., Harms, R., 2018. Searching for startups: Search strategies, search effectiveness and radical innovation capabilities

This paper is under review at Technovation. An earlier version was presented at the XXIX ISPIM conference in Stockholm, Sweden, June 2018.

Chapter 5. Simon, F., Harms, R., Schiele, H., 2017. Managing corporate-startup relationships: What matters for entrepreneurs?

This paper is accepted for publication at the International Journal of Entrepreneurial Venturing and in press (DOI: 10.1504/IJEV.2018.10012021).

A prior version was presented at the 26th IPSERA conference in Balatonfured, Hungary, April 2017 and during the IFPSM summer school, University of Twente, Netherlands, June 2016.

8. References

Agarwal, R., & Helfat, C. E. (2009). Strategic renewal of organizations. *Organization Science, 20*(2), 281-293.

Ahuja, G. (2000). The duality of collaboration: Inducements and opportunities in the formation of interfirm linkages. *Strategic Management Journal, 21*(3), 317-343.

Ahuja, G., & Katila, R. (2001). Technological acquisitions and the innovation performance of acquiring firms: A longitudinal study. *Strategic Management Journal, 22*(3), 197-220.

Al-Zu'bi, Z. b. M., & Tsinopoulos, C. (2012). Suppliers versus lead users: Examining their relative impact on product variety. *Journal of Product Innovation Management, 29*(4), 667-680.

Aldrich, H. E., & Ruef, M. (2006). *Organizations Evolving*. London: SAGE.

Alvarez, S. A., & Barney, J. B. (2001). How entrepreneurial firms can benefit from alliances with large partners. *The Academy of Management Executive, 15*(1), 139-148.

Alvarez, S. A., & Barney, J. B. (2004). Organizing rent generation and appropriation: Toward a theory of the entrepreneurial firm. *Journal of Business Venturing, 19*(5), 621-635.

Amabile, T. M. (1982). Social psychology of creativity: A consensual assessment technique. *Journal of Personality and Social Psychology, 43*(5), 997.

Amabile, T. M., Conti, R., Coon, H., Lazenby, J., & Herron, M. (1996). Assessing the work environment for creativity. *Academy of Management Journal, 39*(5), 1154-1184.

Ancona, D. G., & Caldwell, D. F. (1988). Beyond task and maintenance: Defining external functions in groups. *Group & Organization Studies, 13*(4), 468-494.

Ancona, D. G., & Caldwell, D. F. (1992). Bridging the boundary: External activity and performance in organizational teams. *Administrative Science Quarterly, 37*(4), 634-665.

Anderson, P., & Tushman, M. L. (1990). Technological discontinuities and dominant designs: A cyclical model of technological change. *Administrative Science Quarterly, 35*(4), 604-633.

Andersson, M., & Xiao, J. (2016). Acquisitions of start-ups by incumbent businesses: A market selection process of "high-quality" entrants? *Research Policy, 45*(1), 272-290.

Armstrong, J. S., & Overton, T. S. (1977). Estimating nonresponse bias in mail surveys. *Journal of Marketing Research, 14*(3), 396-402.

Audia, P. G., & Goncalo, J. A. (2007). Past success and creativity over time: A study of inventors in the hard disk drive industry. *Management Science, 53*(1), 1-15.

Audretsch, D. B., Segarra, A., & Teruel, M. (2014). Why don't all young firms invest in R&D? *Small Business Economics, 43*(4), 751-766.

Baker, T., Miner, A. S., & Eesley, D. T. (2003). Improvising firms: Bricolage, account giving and improvisational competencies in the founding process. *Research Policy, 32*(2), 255-276.

Baker, T., & Nelson, R. E. (2005). Creating something from nothing: Resource construction through entrepreneurial bricolage. *Administrative Science Quarterly, 50*(3), 329-366.

Baldwin, C. Y., & Clark, K. B. (2000). *Design rules: The power of modularity*. Cambridge, MA: MIT Press.

Balka, K., Raasch, C., & Herstatt, C. (2014). The effect of selective openness on value creation in user innovation communities. *Journal of Product Innovation Management, 31*(2), 392-407.

Basu, S., Phelps, C. C., & Kotha, S. (2016). Search and integration in external venturing: An inductive examination of corporate venture capital units. *Strategic Entrepreneurship Journal, 10*(2), 129-152.

Benson, D., & Ziedonis, R. H. (2009). Corporate venture capital as a window on new technologies: Implications for the performance of corporate investors when acquiring startups. *Organization Science, 20*(2), 329-351.

Bergek, A., Berggren, C., Magnusson, T., & Hobday, M. (2013). Technological discontinuities and the challenge for incumbent firms: Destruction, disruption or creative accumulation? *Research Policy, 42*(6), 1210-1224.

Bergek, A., & Norrman, C. (2008). Incubator best practice: A framework. *Technovation, 28*(1), 20-28.

Bilgram, V., Brem, A., & Voigt, K.-I. (2008). User-centric innovations in new product development - systematic identification of lead users harnessing interactive and collaborative online-tools. *International Journal of Innovation Management, 12*(3), 419-458.

Bingham, C. B., & Davis, J. P. (2012). Learning sequences: Their existence, effect, and evolution. *Academy of Management Journal, 55*(3), 611-641.

Björk, J., & Magnusson, M. (2009). Where do good innovation ideas come from? Exploring the influence of network connectivity on innovation idea quality. *Journal of Product Innovation Management, 26*(6), 662-670.

Blank, S. (2013). Why the lean start-up changes everything. *Harvard Business Review, 91*(5), 63-72.

Blau, J. (2015). Apple and Google Hope to Slide Into the Driver's Seat. *Research-Technology Management, 58*(4), 5A.

Bogers, M., Zobel, A.-K., Afuah, A., Almirall, E., Brunswicker, S., Dahlander, L., . . . Haefliger, S. (2017). The open innovation research landscape: Established perspectives and emerging themes across different levels of analysis. *Industry and Innovation, 24*(1), 8-40.

Boudreau, K. J., Lacetera, N., & Lakhani, K. R. (2011). Incentives and problem uncertainty in innovation contests: An empirical analysis. *Management Science, 57*(5), 843-863.

Bouncken, R. B. (2015). Ambiguity and knowledge transfer in innovation alliances. *International Journal of Entrepreneurial Venturing, 7*(4), 309-323.

Brunswicker, S., & Hutschek, U. (2010). Crossing horizons: Leveraging cross-industry innovation search in the front-end of the innovation process. *International Journal of Innovation Management, 14*(4), 683-702.

Brusoni, S., Prencipe, A., & Pavitt, K. (2001). Knowledge specialization, organizational coupling, and the boundaries of the firm: Why do firms know more than they make? *Administrative Science Quarterly, 46*(4), 597-621.

Cabigiosu, A., Zirpoli, F., & Camuffo, A. (2013). Modularity, interfaces definition and the integration of external sources of innovation in the automotive industry. *Research Policy, 42*(3), 662-675.

Cassiman, B., & Veugelers, R. (2006). In search of complementarity in innovation strategy: Internal R&D and external knowledge acquisition. *Management Science, 52*(1), 68-82.

Chandy, R. K., & Tellis, G. J. (1998). Organizing for radical product innovation: The overlooked role of willingness to cannibalize. *Journal of Marketing Research, 35*(4), 474-487.

Chandy, R. K., & Tellis, G. J. (2000). The incumbent's curse? Incumbency, size, and radical product innovation. *Journal of Marketing, 64*(3), 1-17.

Chang, S.-J., Van Witteloostuijn, A., & Eden, L. (2010). From the editors: Common method variance in international business research. *Journal of International Business Studies, 41*(2), 178-184.

Chang, Y.-C., Chang, H.-T., Chi, H.-R., Chen, M.-H., & Deng, L.-L. (2012). How do established firms improve radical innovation performance? The organizational capabilities view. *Technovation, 32*(7–8), 441-451.

Chen, H., & Chen, T.-J. (2002). Asymmetric strategic alliances: A network view. *Journal of Business Research, 55*(12), 1007-1013.

Chen, J., Chen, Y., & Vanhaverbeke, W. (2011). The influence of scope, depth, and orientation of external technology sources on the innovative performance of Chinese firms. *Technovation, 31*(8), 362-373.

Chen, Y., Vanhaverbeke, W., & Du, J. (2016). The interaction between internal R&D and different types of external knowledge sourcing: an empirical study of Chinese innovative firms. *R&D Management, 46*(S3), 1006-1023.

Chesbrough, H. W. (2003). *Open innovation: The new imperative for creating and profiting from technology* (First ed.). Boston, MA: Harvard Business School Press.

Chesbrough, H. W., & Brunswicker, S. (2014). A fad or a phenomenon? The adoption of open innovation practices in large firms. *Research-Technology Management, 57*(2), 16-25.

Chiang, Y. H., & Hung, K. P. (2010). Exploring open search strategies and perceived innovation performance from the perspective of inter-organizational knowledge flows. *R&D Management, 40*(3), 292-299.

Chrisman, J. J., Bauerschmidt, A., & Hofer, C. W. (1998). The determinants of new venture performance: An extended model. *Entrepreneurship Theory and Practice, 23*, 5-30.

Christensen, C. M. (1997). *The innovators' dilemma: When new technologies cause great firms to fail.* Boston, MA: Harvard Business Review Press.

Christensen, C. M., & Bower, J. L. (1996). Customer power, strategic investment, and the failure of leading firms. *Strategic Management Journal, 17*(3), 197-218.

Clark, K. B. (1989). Project scope and project performance: The effect of parts strategy and supplier involvement on product development. *Management Science, 35*(10), 1247-1263.

Cohen, W. M., & Levinthal, D. A. (1990). Absorptive capacity: A new perspective on learning and innovation. *Administrative Science Quarterly, 35*(1), 128-152.

Colombo, M. G., von Krogh, G., Rossi-Lamastra, C., & Stephan, P. E. (2017). Organizing for Radical Innovation: Exploring Novel Insights. *Journal of Product Innovation Management, 34*(4), 394-405.

Cooper, A. C. (1981). Strategic management: New ventures and small business. *Long Range Planning, 14*(5), 39-45.

Cooper, R. G. (1990). Stage-gate systems: A new tool for managing new products. *Business Horizons, 33*(3), 44-54.

Cooper, R. G. (2008). Perspective: The stage-gate idea-to-launch process—update, what's new, and nexgen systems. *Journal of Product Innovation Management, 25*(3), 213-232.

Criscuolo, P., Laursen, K., Reichstein, T., & Salter, A. (2018). Winning combinations: Search strategies and innovativeness in the UK. *Industry and Innovation, 25*(2), 115-143.

Criscuolo, P., Nicolaou, N., & Salter, A. (2012). The elixir (or burden) of youth? Exploring differences in innovation between start-ups and established firms. *Research Policy, 41*(2), 319-333.

Cruz-González, J., López-Sáez, P., Navas-López, J. E., & Delgado-Verde, M. (2015). Open search strategies and firm performance: The different moderating role of technological environmental dynamism. *Technovation, 35*, 32-45.

Dahlander, L., & Gann, D. M. (2010). How open is innovation? *Research policy, 39*(6), 699-709.

Dahlstrand, Å. L. (1997). Growth and inventiveness in technology-based spin-off firms. *Research Policy, 26*(3), 331-344.

Das, T. K., & Teng, B.-S. (2002). Alliance constellations: A social exchange perspective. *Academy of Management Review, 27*(3), 445-456.

De Meyer, A. (1999). Using strategic partnerships to create a sustainable competitive position for hi-tech start-up firms. *R&D Management, 29*(4), 323-328.

DeCarolis, D. M., & Deeds, D. L. (1999). The impact of stocks and flows of organizational knowledge on firm performance: An empirical investigation of the biotechnology industry. *Strategic Management Journal, 20*(10), 953-968.

Deeds, D. L., & Hill, C. W. (1996). Strategic alliances and the rate of new product development: An empirical study of entrepreneurial biotechnology firms. *Journal of Business Venturing, 11*(1), 41-55.

Diestre, L., & Rajagopalan, N. (2012). Are all 'sharks' dangerous? New biotechnology ventures and partner selection in R&D alliances. *Strategic Management Journal, 33*(10), 1115-1134.

Dillman, D. A. (2006). *Mail and Internet surveys: The tailored design method.* Hoboken, NJ: Wiley.

Dollinger, M. J. (1984). Environmental boundary spanning and information processing effects on organizational performance. *Academy of Management Journal, 27*(2), 351-368.

Dosi, G., Faillo, M., & Marengo, L. (2008). Organizational capabilities, patterns of knowledge accumulation and governance structures in business firms: An introduction. London: SAGE.

Doz, Y. L. (1987). Technology partnerships between larger and smaller firms: Some critical issues. *International Studies of Management & Organization, 17*(4), 31-57.

Doz, Y. L., & Hamel, G. (1998). *Alliance advantage: The art of creating value through partnering* (First ed.). Boston, MA: Harvard Business School Press.

Doz, Y. L., Santos, J., & Williamson, P. J. (2001). *From global to metanational: How companies win in the knowledge economy.* Boston, MA: Harvard Business School Press.

Dushnitsky, G., & Lenox, M. J. (2005). When do incumbents learn from entrepreneurial ventures? Corporate venture capital and investing firm innovation rates. *Research Policy, 34*(5), 615-639.

Dushnitsky, G., & Lenox, M. J. (2006). When does corporate venture capital investment create firm value? *Journal of Business Venturing, 21*(6), 753-772.

Dushnitsky, G., & Shapira, Z. (2010). Entrepreneurial finance meets organizational reality: Comparing investment practices and performance of corporate and independent venture capitalists. *Strategic Management Journal, 31*(9), 990-1017.

Dyer, J. H., & Nobeoka, K. (2000). Creating and managing a high-performance knowledge-sharing network: The Toyota case. *Strategic Management Journal, 21*(3), 345-367.

Efron, B., & Tibshirani, R. J. (1994). *An introduction to the bootstrap.* London: Chapman and Hall.

Eisenhardt, K. M. (1989). Building theories from case study research. *Academy of Management Review, 14*(4), 532-550.

Eisenhardt, K. M., & Graebner, M. E. (2007). Theory building from cases: Opportunities and challenges. *Academy of Management Journal, 50*(1), 25-32.

Eisenhardt, K. M., & Martin, J. A. (2000). Dynamic capabilities: What are they? *Strategic Management Journal, 21*(10/11), 1105-1121.

Engel, J. S. (2011). Accelerating corporate innovation: Lessons from the venture capital model. *Research-Technology Management, 54*(3), 36-43.

Fauchart, E., & Gruber, M. (2011). Darwinians, communitarians, and missionaries: The role of founder identity in entrepreneurship. *Academy of Management Journal, 54*(5), 935-957.

Felin, T., & Zenger, T. R. (2014). Closed or open innovation? Problem solving and the governance choice. *Research Policy, 43*(5), 914-925.

Fischer, T., & Henkel, J. (2013). Complements and substitutes in profiting from innovation— A choice experimental approach. *Research Policy, 42*(2), 326-339.

Fjeldstad, Ø. D., Snow, C. C., Miles, R. E., & Lettl, C. (2012). The architecture of collaboration. *Strategic Management Journal, 33*(6), 734-750.

Fleming, L., & Sorenson, O. (2001). Technology as a complex adaptive system: Evidence from patent data. *Research Policy, 30*(7), 1019-1039.

Fleming, L., & Sorenson, O. (2004). Science as a map in technological search. *Strategic Management Journal, 25*(8-9), 909-928.

Flick, U. (2009). *An introduction to qualitative research* (Fourth ed.). London: SAGE.

Foddy, W. (1994). *Constructing questions for interviews and questionnaires: Theory and practice in social research.* Cambridge: Cambridge University Press.

Fombrun, C., & Shanley, M. (1990). What's in a name? Reputation building and corporate strategy. *Academy of Management Journal, 33*(2), 233-258.

Franke, N., Poetz, M. K., & Schreier, M. (2014). Integrating problem solvers from analogous markets in new product ideation. *Management Science, 60*(4), 1063-1081.

Freeman, J., & Engel, J. S. (2007). Models of innovation. *California Management Review, 50*(1), 94-119.

Füller, J., Hutter, K., Hautz, J., & Matzler, K. (2017). The role of professionalism in innovation contest communities. *Long Range Planning, 50*(2), 243-259.

Gao, G. Y., Xie, E., & Zhou, K. Z. (2015). How does technological diversity in supplier network drive buyer innovation? Relational process and contingencies. *Journal of Operations Management, 36*, 165-177.

Garrido, E. A., & Dushnitsky, G. (2016). Are entrepreneurial venture's innovation rates sensitive to investor complementary assets? Comparing biotech ventures backed by corporate and independent VCs. *Strategic Management Journal, 37*(5), 819-834.

Gassmann, O., & Gaso, B. (2004). Insourcing creativity with listening posts in decentralized firms. *Creativity and Innovation Management, 13*(1), 3-14.

Gassmann, O., Zeschky, M., Wolff, T., & Stahl, M. (2010). Crossing the industry-line: Breakthrough innovation through cross-industry alliances with 'non-suppliers'. *Long Range Planning, 43*(5), 639-654.

Gavetti, G., & Levinthal, D. (2000). Looking forward and looking backward: Cognitive and experiential search. *Administrative Science Quarterly, 45*(1), 113-137.

George, J. M. (2007). Creativity in Organizations. *Academy of Management Annals, 1*(1), 439-477.

Gerlach, S., & Brem, A. (2015). What determines a successful business incubator? Introduction to an incubator guide. *International Journal of Entrepreneurial Venturing, 7*(3), 286-307.

Gioia, D. A., Corley, K. G., & Hamilton, A. L. (2013). Seeking qualitative rigor in inductive research: Notes on the Gioia methodology. *Organizational Research Methods, 16*(1), 15-31.

Giones, F., & Brem, A. (2017). Digital Technology Entrepreneurship: A Definition and Research Agenda. *Technology Innovation Management Review, 7*(5), 44-51.

Grant, R. M. (1996a). Prospering in dynamically-competitive environments: Organizational capability as knowledge integration. *Organization Science, 7*(4), 375-387.

Grant, R. M. (1996b). Toward a knowledge-based theory of the firm. *Strategic Management Journal, 17*(S2), 109-122.

Gulati, R., & Singh, H. (1998). The architecture of cooperation: Managing coordination costs and appropriation concerns in strategic alliances. *Administrative Science Quarterly, 43*(4), 781-814.

Hagedoorn, J., & Duysters, G. (2002). External sources of innovative capabilities: The preferences for strategic alliances or mergers and acquisitions. *Journal of Management Studies, 39*(2), 167-188.

Hair, J. F., Black, W. C., Babin, B. J., Anderson, R. E., & Tatham, R. L. (2006). *Multivariate data analysis.* Upper Saddle River, NJ: Pearson Prentice Hallhall

Harman, H. H. (1976). *Modern factor analysis.* Chicago, IL: University of Chicago Press.

Harrison, J. S., Hitt, M. A., Hoskisson, R. E., & Ireland, R. D. (2001). Resource complementarity in business combinations: Extending the logic to organizational alliances. *Journal of Management, 27*(6), 679-690.

Helfat, C. E., & Martin, J. A. (2015). Dynamic managerial capabilities: Review and assessment of managerial impact on strategic change. *Journal of Management, 41*(5), 1281-1312.

Henderson, R. (1993). Underinvestment and incompetence as responses to radical innovation: Evidence from the photolithographic alignment equipment industry. *The RAND Journal of Economics, 24*(2), 248-270.

Hill, S. A., & Birkinshaw, J. (2014). Ambidexterity and survival in corporate venture units. *Journal of Management, 40*(7), 1899-1931.

Hillman, A. J., Withers, M. C., & Collins, B. J. (2009). Resource dependence theory: A review. *Journal of Management, 35*(6), 1404 –1427.

Hoenig, D., & Henkel, J. (2015). Quality signals? The role of patents, alliances, and team experience in venture capital financing. *Research Policy, 44*(5), 1049-1064.

Homfeldt, F., Rese, A., Brenner, H., Baier, D., & Schäfer, T. F. (2017). Identification and Generation of Innovative Ideas in the Procurement of the Automotive Industry: The Case of AUDI AG. *International Journal of Innovation Management, 21*(7), 1750053 (1750031 pages).

Hora, M., & Dutta, D. K. (2013). Entrepreneurial firms and downstream alliance partnerships: Impact of portfolio depth and scope on technology innovation and commercialization success. *Production and Operations Management, 22*(6), 1389-1400.

Hüttinger, L., Schiele, H., & Schröer, D. (2014). Exploring the antecedents of preferential customer treatment by suppliers: a mixed methods approach. *Supply Chain Management: An International Journal, 19*(5/6), 697-721.

Ili, S., Albers, A., & Miller, S. (2010). Open innovation in the automotive industry. *R&D Management, 40*(3), 246-255.

Inkpen, A. C., & Currall, S. C. (2004). The coevolution of trust, control, and learning in joint ventures. *Organization Science, 15*(5), 586-599.

Ireland, R. D., Hitt, M. A., & Sirmon, D. G. (2003). A model of strategic entrepreneurship: The construct and its dimensions. *Journal of Management, 29*(6), 963-989.

Ireland, R. D., & Webb, J. W. (2007). A cross-disciplinary exploration of entrepreneurship research. *Journal of Management, 33*(6), 891-927.

John, G., & Reve, T. (1982). The reliability and validity of key informant data from dyadic relationships in marketing channels. *Journal of Marketing Research, 19*(4), 517-524.

Johnsen, T. E. (2009). Supplier involvement in new product development and innovation: Taking stock and looking to the future. *Journal of Purchasing and Supply Management, 15*(3), 187-197.

Kalaignanam, K., Shankar, V., & Varadarajan, R. (2007). Asymmetric new product development alliances: Win-win or win-lose partnerships? *Management Science, 53*(3), 357-374.

Katila, R., & Ahuja, G. (2002). Something old, something new: A longitudinal study of search behavior and new product introduction. *Academy of Management Journal, 45*(6), 1183-1194.

Katila, R., Rosenberger, J. D., & Eisenhardt, K. M. (2008). Swimming with sharks: Technology ventures, defense mechanisms and corporate relationships. *Administrative Science Quarterly, 53*(2), 295-332.

Katila, R., & Shane, S. (2005). When does lack of resources make new firms innovative? *Academy of Management Journal, 48*(5), 814-829.

Katz, R., & Allen, T. J. (1982). Investigating the not invented here (NIH) syndrome: A look at the performance, tenure, and communication patterns of 50 R&D project groups. *R&D Management, 12*(1), 7-20.

Kazanjian, R. K. (1988). Relation of dominant problems to stages of growth in technology-based new ventures. *Academy of Management Journal, 31*(2), 257-279.

Keil, T., Maula, M., Schildt, H., & Zahra, S. A. (2008). The effect of governance modes and relatedness of external business development activities on innovative performance. *Strategic Management Journal, 29*(8), 895-907.

Kickul, J. R., Griffiths, M. D., Jayaram, J., & Wagner, S. M. (2011). Operations management, entrepreneurship, and value creation: Emerging opportunities in a cross-disciplinary context. *Journal of Operations Management, 29*, 78–85.

Kim, J., & Wilemon, D. (2002). Focusing the fuzzy front–end in new product development. *R&D Management, 32*(4), 269-279.

Knudsen, T., & Srikanth, K. (2014). Coordinated exploration organizing joint search by multiple specialists to overcome mutual confusion and joint myopia. *Administrative Science Quarterly, 59*(3), 409-441.

Kock, A., Heising, W., & Gemünden, H. G. (2015). How ideation portfolio management influences front-end success. *Journal of Product Innovation Management, 32*(4), 539-555.

Kogut, B., & Zander, U. (1992). Knowledge of the firm, combinative capabilities, and the replication of technology. *Organization Science, 3*(3), 383-397.

Köhler, C., Sofka, W., & Grimpe, C. (2012). Selective search, sectoral patterns, and the impact on product innovation performance. *Research Policy, 41*(8), 1344-1356.

Kohler, T. (2016). Corporate accelerators: Building bridges between corporations and startups. *Business Horizons, 59*(3), 347-357.

Koufteros, X., Vonderembse, M., & Jayaram, J. (2005). Internal and external integration for product development: The contingency effects of uncertainty, equivocality, and platform strategy. *Decision Sciences, 36*(1), 97-133.

Kutner, M. H., Nachtsheim, C., & Neter, J. (2004). *Applied linear regression models.* Columbus, OH: McGraw-Hill Higher Education.

LaBahn, D. W., & Krapfel, R. (2000). Early supplier involvement in customer new product development: A contingency model of component supplier intentions. *Journal of Business Research, 47*(3), 173-190.

Lakemond, N., Bengtsson, L., Laursen, K., & Tell, F. (2016). Match and manage: The use of knowledge matching and project management to integrate knowledge in collaborative inbound open innovation. *Industrial and Corporate Change, 25*(2), 333-352.

Langner, B., & Seidel, V. P. (2009). Collaborative concept development using supplier competitions: Insights from the automotive industry. *Journal of Engineering and Technology Management, 26*(1), 1-14.

Larson, A. (1992). Network dyads in entrepreneurial settings: A study of the governance of exchange relationships. *Administrative Science Quarterly, 37*(1), 76-104.

Lau, A. K., Tang, E., & Yam, R. (2010). Effects of supplier and customer integration on product innovation and performance: Empirical evidence in Hong Kong manufacturers. *Journal of Product Innovation Management, 27*(5), 761-777.

Laursen, K. (2012). Keep searching and you'll find: What do we know about variety creation through firms' search activities for innovation? *Industrial and Corporate Change, 21*(5), 1181-1220.

Laursen, K., Masciarelli, F., & Prencipe, A. (2012). Regions matter: How localized social capital affects innovation and external knowledge acquisition. *Organization Science, 23*(1), 177-193.

Laursen, K., & Salter, A. J. (2006). Open for innovation: The role of openness in explaining innovation performance among UK manufacturing firms. *Strategic Management Journal, 27*(2), 131-150.

Laursen, K., & Salter, A. J. (2014). The paradox of openness: Appropriability, external search and collaboration. *Research Policy, 43*(5), 867-878.

Lavie, D. (2007). Alliance portfolios and firm performance: A study of value creation and appropriation in the US software industry. *Strategic Management Journal, 28*(12), 1187-1212.

Lavie, D., & Rosenkopf, L. (2006). Balancing exploration and exploitation in alliance formation. *Academy of Management Journal, 49*(4), 797-818.

Lawson, B., & Samson, D. (2001). Developing innovation capability in organisations: A dynamic capabilities approach. *International Journal of Innovation Management, 5*(3), 377-400.

Leana, C. R., & Van Buren, H. J. (1999). Organizational social capital and employment practices. *Academy of Management Review, 24*(3), 538-555.

Lee, C., Lee, K., & Pennings, J. M. (2001). Internal capabilities, external networks, and performance: A study on technology-based ventures. *Strategic Management Journal, 22*(6-7), 615-640.

Leifer, R., & Delbecq, A. (1978). Organizational/environmental interchange: A model of boundary spanning activity. *Academy of Management Review, 3*(1), 40-50.

Leiponen, A., & Helfat, C. E. (2010). Innovation objectives, knowledge sources, and the benefits of breadth. *Strategic Management Journal, 31*(2), 224-236.

Levinthal, D. A., & March, J. G. (1993). The myopia of learning. *Strategic Management Journal, 14*(S2), 95-112.

Levitt, T. (1963). Creativity is not enough. *Harvard Business Review, 41*(3), 72-83.

Li, D., Eden, L., Hitt, M. A., & Ireland, R. D. (2008). Friends, acquaintances, or strangers? Partner selection in R&D alliances. *Academy of Management Journal, 51*(2), 315-334.

Liang, H., Saraf, N., Hu, Q., & Xue, Y. (2007). Assimilation of enterprise systems: The effect of institutional pressures and the mediating role of top management. *MIS Quarterly, 31*(1), 59-87.

Lichtenthaler, E. (2005). Corporate diversification: Identifying new businesses systematically in the diversified firm. *Technovation, 25*(7), 697-709.

Lilien, G. L., Morrison, P. D., Searls, K., Sonnack, M., & Hippel, E. v. (2002). Performance assessment of the lead user idea-generation process for new product development. *Management Science, 48*(8), 1042-1059.

Linton, J. D., & Solomon, G. T. (2017). Technology, innovation, entrepreneurship and the small business - technology and innovation in small business. *Journal of Small Business Management, 55*(2), 196-199.

Lopez-Vega, H., Tell, F., & Vanhaverbeke, W. (2016). Where and how to search? Search paths in open innovation. *Research Policy, 45*(1), 125-136.

Love, J. H., Roper, S., & Vahter, P. (2014). Learning from openness: The dynamics of breadth in external innovation linkages. *Strategic Management Journal, 35*(11), 1703-1716.

Lumpkin, G. T., & Dess, G. G. (1996). Clarifying the entrepreneurial orientation construct and linking it to performance. *Academy of Management Review, 21*(1), 135-172.

Luzzini, D., Amann, M., Caniato, F., Essig, M., & Ronchi, S. (2015). The path of innovation: Purchasing and supplier involvement into new product development. *Industrial Marketing Management, 47*, 109-120.

Maggitti, P. G., Smith, K. G., & Katila, R. (2013). The complex search process of invention. *Research Policy, 42*(1), 90-100.

Magnusson, P. R. (2009). Exploring the contributions of involving ordinary users in ideation of technology-based services. *Journal of Product Innovation Management, 26*(5), 578-593.

March, J. G. (1991). Exploration and exploitation in organizational learning. *Organization Science, 2*(1), 71-87.

Marion, T. J., Friar, J. H., & Simpson, T. W. (2012). New product development practices and early-stage firms: Two in-depth case studies. *Journal of Product Innovation Management, 29*(4), 639-654.

Martini, A., Neirotti, P., & Appio, F. P. (2017). Knowledge searching, integrating and performing: Always a tuned trio for innovation? *Long Range Planning, 50*(2), 200-220.

McDougall, P. P., Covin, J. G., Robinson, R. B., & Herron, L. (1994). The effects of industry growth and strategic breadth on new venture performance and strategy content. *Strategic Management Journal, 15*(7), 537-554.

Miles, M. B., & Huberman, A. M. (1994). *Qualitative data analysis: An expanded sourcebook* (Second ed.). Thousand Oaks, CA: SAGE.

Minshall, T., Mortara, L., Elia, S., & Probert, D. (2008). Development of practitioner guidelines for partnerships between start-ups and large firms. *Journal of Manufacturing Technology Management, 19*(3), 391-406.

Minshall, T., Mortara, L., Valli, R., & Probert, D. (2010). Making "asymmetric" partnerships work. *Research-Technology Management, 53*(3), 53-63.

Mitchell, W., & Singh, K. (1992). Incumbents' use of pre-entry alliances before expansion into new technical subfields of an industry. *Journal of Economic Behavior & Organization, 18*(3), 347-372.

Mohr, J., & Spekman, R. (1994). Characteristics of partnership success: Partnership attributes, communication behavior, and conflict resolution techniques. *Strategic Management Journal, 15*(2), 135-152.

Monteiro, F., & Birkinshaw, J. (2017). The external knowledge sourcing process in multinational corporations. *Strategic Management Journal, 38*(2), 342-362.

Monteiro, F., Mol, M., & Birkinshaw, J. (2017). Ready to be open? Explaining the firm level barriers to benefiting from openness to external knowledge. *Long Range Planning, 50*(2), 282-295.

Moreau, C. P., & Dahl, D. W. (2005). Designing the solution: The impact of constraints on consumers' creativity. *Journal of Consumer Research, 32*(1), 13-22.

Moreau, C. P., Lehmann, D. R., & Markman, A. B. (2001). Entrenched knowledge structures and consumer response to new products. *Journal of Marketing Research, 38*(1), 14-29.

Nambisan, S. (2017). Digital entrepreneurship: Toward a digital technology perspective of entrepreneurship. *Entrepreneurship Theory and Practice, 41*(6), 1029–1055.

Nambisan, S., & Sawhney, M. (2007). A buyer's guide to the innovation bazaar. *Harvard Business Review, 85*(6), 109-118.

Narayanan, V., Yang, Y., & Zahra, S. A. (2009). Corporate venturing and value creation: A review and proposed framework. *Research Policy, 38*(1), 58-76.

Nelson, R. R. (1961). Uncertainty, learning, and the economics of parallel research and development efforts. *The Review of Economics and Statistics, 43*(4), 351-364.

Nickerson, J. A., & Zenger, T. R. (2004). A knowledge-based theory of the firm - The problem-solving perspective. *Organization Science, 15*(6), 617-632.

Nonaka, I. (1994). A dynamic theory of organizational knowledge creation. *Organization Science, 5*(1), 14-37.

O'Connor, G. C., & Ayers, A. (2005). Building a radical innovation competency. *Research-Technology Management, 48*(1), 23-31.

O'Connor, G. C., & De Martino, R. (2006). Organizing for radical innovation: An exploratory study of the structural aspects of RI management systems in large established firms. *Journal of Product Innovation Management, 23*(6), 475-497.

O'Connor, G. C., & Rice, M. P. (2013). A comprehensive model of uncertainty associated with radical innovation. *Journal of Product Innovation Management, 30*(S1), 2-18.

Park, H. D., & Steensma, H. K. (2012). When does corporate venture capital add value for new ventures? *Strategic Management Journal, 33*(1), 1-22.

Parmigiani, A., & Rivera-Santos, M. (2011). Clearing a path through the forest: A meta-review of interorganizational relationships. *Journal of Management, 37*(4), 1108-1136.

Patton, M. Q. (2002). *Qualitative research* (Third ed.). Thousand Oaks, CA: Wiley.

Pauwels, C., Clarysse, B., Wright, M., & Van Hove, J. (2016). Understanding a new generation incubation model: The accelerator. *Technovation, 50*, 13-24.

Penrose, E. T. (1959). *The Theory of the Growth of the Firm* (First ed.). New York, NY: Wiley.

Perols, J., Zimmermann, C., & Kortmann, S. (2013). On the relationship between supplier integration and time-to-market. *Journal of Operations Management, 31*(3), 153-167.

Pfeffer, J., & Salancik, G. (1978). *The external control of organizations: A resource dependence perspective* (First ed.). New York, NY: Harper & Row.

Phillips, W., Lamming, R., Bessant, J., & Noke, H. (2006). Discontinuous innovation and supply relationships: Strategic dalliances. *R&D Management, 36*(4), 451-461.

Podsakoff, P. M., MacKenzie, S. B., Lee, J.-Y., & Podsakoff, N. P. (2003). Common method biases in behavioral research: A critical review of the literature and recommended remedies. *Journal of Applied Psychology, 88*(5), 879-903.

Poetz, M. K., & Schreier, M. (2012). The value of crowdsourcing: Can users really compete with professionals in generating new product ideas? *Journal of Product Innovation Management, 29*(2), 245-256.

Powell, W. W., Koput, K. W., & Smith-Doerr, L. (1996). Interorganizational collaboration and the locus of innovation: Networks of learning in biotechnology. *Administrative Science Quarterly, 41*(1), 116-145.

Prashantham, S., & Birkinshaw, J. (2008). Dancing with gorillas: How small companies can partner effectively with MNCs. *California Management Review, 51*(1), 6-23.

Primo, M. A., & Amundson, S. D. (2002). An exploratory study of the effects of supplier relationships on new product development outcomes. *Journal of Operations Management, 20*(1), 33-52.

Pulles, N. J., Schiele, H., Veldman, J., & Hüttinger, L. (2016). The impact of customer attractiveness and supplier satisfaction on becoming a preferred customer. *Industrial Marketing Management, 54*, 129-140.

Pulles, N. J., Veldman, J., & Schiele, H. (2014). Identifying innovative suppliers in business networks: An empirical study. *Industrial Marketing Management, 43*(3), 409-418.

Ragatz, G. L., Handfield, R. B., & Scannell, T. V. (1997). Success factors for integrating suppliers into new product development. *Journal of Product Innovation Management, 14*(3), 190-202.

Randhawa, K., Wilden, R., & Hohberger, J. (2016). A bibliometric review of open innovation: Setting a research agenda. *Journal of Product Innovation Management, 33*(6), 750-772.

Reinartz, W., Haenlein, M., & Henseler, J. (2009). An empirical comparison of the efficacy of covariance-based and variance-based SEM. *International Journal of Research in Marketing, 26*(4), 332-344.

Rese, A., Sänn, A., & Homfeldt, F. (2015). Customer integration and voice–of–customer methods in the German automotive industry. *International Journal of Automotive Technology and Management, 15*(1), 1-19.

Richter, C., Kraus, S., Brem, A., Durst, S., & Giselbrecht, C. (2017). Digital entrepreneurship: Innovative business models for the sharing economy. *Creativity and Innovation Management, 26*(3), 300-310.

Ries, E. (2011). *The lean startup: How today's entrepreneurs use continuous innovation to create radically successful businesses*. New York, NY: Random House Digital.

Rohrbeck, R. (2010). Harnessing a network of experts for competitive advantage: Technology scouting in the ICT industry. *R&D Management, 40*(2), 169-180.

Rohrbeck, R., Hölzle, K., & Gemünden, H. G. (2009). Opening up for competitive advantage– How Deutsche Telekom creates an open innovation ecosystem. *R&D Management, 39*(4), 420-430.

Rosenkopf, L., & Almeida, P. (2003). Overcoming local search through alliances and mobility. *Management Science, 49*(6), 751-766.

Rosenkopf, L., & Nerkar, A. (2001). Beyond local search: Boundary-spanning, exploration, and impact in the optical disk industry. *Strategic Management Journal, 22*(4), 287-306.

Rothaermel, F. T. (2002). Technological discontinuities and interfirm cooperation: What determines a startup's attractiveness as alliance partner? *IEEE Transactions on Engineering Management, 49*(4), 388-397.

Rothaermel, F. T., & Alexandre, M. T. (2009). Ambidexterity in technology sourcing: The moderating role of absorptive capacity. *Organization Science, 20*(4), 759-780.

Salerno, M. S., de Vasconcelos Gomes, L. A., da Silva, D. O., Bagno, R. B., & Freitas, S. L. T. U. (2015). Innovation processes: Which process for which project? *Technovation, 35*, 59-70.

Salter, A., Wal, A. L., Criscuolo, P., & Alexy, O. (2015). Open for ideation: Individual-level openness and idea generation in R&D. *Journal of Product Innovation Management, 32*(4), 488-504.

Santoro, M. D., & McGill, J. P. (2005). The effect of uncertainty and asset co-specialization on governance in biotechnology alliances. *Strategic Management Journal, 26*(13), 1261-1269.

Santos, F. M., & Eisenhardt, K. M. (2009). Constructing markets and shaping boundaries: Entrepreneurial power in nascent fields. *Academy of Management Journal, 52*(4), 643-671.

Sapienza, H. J., Autio, E., George, G., & Zahra, S. A. (2006). A capabilities perspective on the effects of early internationalization on firm survival and growth. *Academy of Management Review, 31*(4), 914-933.

Schafer, J. L., & Graham, J. W. (2002). Missing data: Our view of the state of the art. *Psychological Methods, 7*(2), 147.

Schemmann, B., Herrmann, A. M., Chappin, M. M., & Heimeriks, G. J. (2016). Crowdsourcing ideas: Involving ordinary users in the ideation phase of new product development. *Research Policy, 45*(6), 1145-1154.

Schiele, H. (2006). How to distinguish innovative suppliers? Identifying innovative suppliers as new task for purchasing. *Industrial Marketing Management, 35*(8), 925-935.

Schiele, H. (2010). Early supplier integration: The dual role of purchasing in new product development. *R&D Management, 40*(2), 138-153.

Schiele, H. (2012). Accessing supplier innovation by being their preferred customer. *Research-Technology Management, 55*(1), 44-50.

Schiele, H., Calvi, R., & Gibbert, M. (2012). Customer attractiveness, supplier satisfaction and preferred customer status: Introduction, definitions and an overarching framework. *Industrial Marketing Management, 41*(8), 1178-1185.

Schiele, H., Horn, P., & Vos, B. (2011). Estimating cost-saving potential from international sourcing and other sourcing levers: Relative importance and trade-offs. *International Journal of Physical Distribution & Logistics Management, 41*(3), 315-336.

Schiele, H., Veldman, J., & Hüttinger, L. (2011). Supplier innovativeness and supplier pricing: The role of preferred customer status. *International Journal of Innovation Management, 15*(01), 1-27.

Schoenherr, T., & Wagner, S. M. (2016). Supplier involvement in the fuzzy front end of new product development: An investigation of homophily, benevolence and market turbulence. *International Journal of Production Economics, 180*, 101-113.

Schoonhoven, C. B., Eisenhardt, K. M., & Lyman, K. (1990). Speeding products to market: Waiting time to first product introduction in new firms. *Administrative Science Quarterly, 35*(1), 177-207.

Schweisfurth, T. G. (2017). Comparing internal and external lead users as sources of innovation. *Research Policy, 46*(1), 238-248.

Shanock, L. R., Baran, B. E., Gentry, W. A., Pattison, S. C., & Heggestad, E. D. (2010). Polynomial regression with response surface analysis: A powerful approach for examining moderation and overcoming limitations of difference scores. *Journal of Business and Psychology, 25*(4), 543-554.

Shrout, P. E., & Fleiss, J. L. (1979). Intraclass correlations: Uses in assessing rater reliability. *Psychological Bulletin, 86*(2), 420-428.

Silverman, D. (2016). *Qualitative research*. Thousand Oaks, CA: SAGE.

Singh, J. V., Tucker, D. J., & House, R. J. (1986). Organizational legitimacy and the liability of newness. *Administrative Science Quarterly, 31*(2), 171-193.

Song, M., & Di Benedetto, C. A. (2008). Supplier's involvement and success of radical new product development in new ventures. *Journal of Operations Management, 26*(1), 1-22.

Song, M., Podoynitsyna, K., Van Der Bij, H., & Halman, J. I. (2008). Success factors in new ventures: A meta-analysis. *Journal of Product Innovation Management, 25*(1), 7-27.

Song, M., & Thieme, J. (2009). The role of suppliers in market intelligence gathering for radical and incremental innovation. *Journal of Product Innovation Management, 26*(1), 43-57.

Souitaris, V., Zerbinati, S., & Liu, G. (2012). Which iron cage? Endo-and exoisomorphism in corporate venture capital programs. *Academy of Management Journal, 55*(2), 477-505.

Steensma, H. K., & Corley, K. G. (2000). On the performance of technology-sourcing partnerships: The interaction between partner interdependence and technology attributes. *Academy of Management Journal, 43*(6), 1045-1067.

Steinle, C., & Schiele, H. (2008). Limits to global sourcing? Strategic consequences of dependency on international suppliers: Cluster theory, resource-based view and case studies. *Journal of Purchasing and Supply Management, 14*(1), 3-14.

Stettner, U., & Lavie, D. (2014). Ambidexterity under scrutiny: Exploration and exploitation via internal organization, alliances, and acquisitions. *Strategic Management Journal, 35*(13), 1903-1929.

Stinchcombe, A. L. (Ed.) (1965). *Social structure and organizations*. Chicago: Rand McNally.

Strauss, A., & Corbin, J. (1998). *Basics of qualitative research: Techniques and procedures for developing grounded theory* (Second ed.). London: SAGE.

Street, C. T., & Cameron, A. F. (2007). External relationships and the small business: A review of small business alliance and network research. *Journal of Small Business Management, 45*(2), 239-266.

Stuart, T. E. (2000). Interorganizational alliances and the performance of firms: A study of growth and innovation rates in a high-technology industry. *Strategic Management Journal, 21*(8), 791-811.

Stuart, T. E., Hoang, H., & Hybels, R. C. (1999). Interorganizational endorsements and the performance of entrepreneurial ventures. *Administrative Science Quarterly, 44*(2), 315-349.

Stuart, T. E., & Podolny, J. M. (1996). Local search and the evolution of technological capabilities. *Strategic Management Journal, 17*(S1), 21-38.

Subramaniam, M., & Youndt, M. A. (2005). The influence of intellectual capital on the types of innovative capabilities. *Academy of Management Journal, 48*(3), 450-463.

Sulej, J. C., Stewart, V., & Keogh, W. (2001). Taking risk in joint ventures: Whose throw of the dice? *Strategic Change, 10*(5), 285-295.

Svahn, F., Mathiassen, L., & Lindgren, R. (2017). Embracing Digital Innovation in Incumbent Firms: How Volvo Cars Managed Competing Concerns. *MIS Quarterly, 41*(1).

Teece, D. J. (1986). Profiting from technological innovation: Implications for integration, collaboration, licensing and public policy. *Research Policy, 15*(6), 285-305.

Terjesen, S., Patel, P. C., & Covin, J. G. (2011). Alliance diversity, environmental context and the value of manufacturing capabilities among new high technology ventures. *Journal of Operations Management, 29*(1), 105-115.

Tripsas, M., & Gavetti, G. (2000). Capabilities, cognition, and inertia: Evidence from digital imaging. *Strategic Management Journal*, 1147-1161.

Tushman, M. L. (1977). Special boundary roles in the innovation process. *Administrative Science Quarterly, 22*(4), 587-605.

Tushman, M. L., & O'Reilly, C. A. (1996). Ambidextrous organizations: Managing evolutionary and revolutionary change. *California Management Review, 38*(4), 8-29.

Tushman, M. L., & Scanlan, T. J. (1981). Boundary spanning individuals: Their role in information transfer and their antecedents. *Academy of Management Journal, 24*(2), 289-305.

Un, C. A., & Asakawa, K. (2015). Types of R&D collaborations and process innovation: The benefit of collaborating upstream in the knowledge chain. *Journal of Product Innovation Management, 32*(1), 138-153.

Un, C. A., Cuervo-Cazurra, A., & Asakawa, K. (2010). R&D collaborations and product innovation. *Journal of Product Innovation Management, 27*(5), 673-689.

Utterback, J. M., & Abernathy, W. J. (1975). A dynamic model of process and product innovation. *Omega, 3*(6), 639-656.

van Burg, E., Podoynitsyna, K., Beck, L., & Lommelen, T. (2012). Directive deficiencies: How resource constraints direct opportunity identification in SMEs. *Journal of Product Innovation Management, 29*(6), 1000-1011.

Van de Vrande, V. (2013). Balancing your technology-sourcing portfolio: How sourcing mode diversity enhances innovative performance. *Strategic Management Journal, 34*(5), 610-621.

Van de Vrande, V., Lemmens, C., & Vanhaverbeke, W. (2006). Choosing governance modes for external technology sourcing. *R&D Management, 36*(3), 347-363.

Van de Vrande, V., Vanhaverbeke, W., & Duysters, G. (2009). External technology sourcing: The effect of uncertainty on governance mode choice. *Journal of Business Venturing, 24*(1), 62-80.

van den Ende, J., Frederiksen, L., & Prencipe, A. (2015). The front end of innovation: Organizing search for ideas. *Journal of Product Innovation Management, 32*(4), 482-487.

van Wijk, R., Jansen, J. J., & Lyles, M. A. (2008). Inter-and intra-organizational knowledge transfer: A meta-analytic review and assessment of its antecedents and consequences. *Journal of Management Studies, 45*(4), 830-853.

Verworn, B. (2009). A structural equation model of the impact of the "fuzzy front end" on the success of new product development. *Research Policy, 38*(10), 1571-1581.

Veugelers, R. (1997). Internal R&D expenditures and external technology sourcing. *Research Policy, 26*(3), 303-315.

Villalonga, B., & McGahan, A. M. (2005). The choice among acquisitions, alliances, and divestitures. *Strategic Management Journal, 26*(13), 1183-1208.

Von Hippel, E. (2005). *Democratizing innovation*. Cambridge, MA: MIT press.

Wadhwa, A., & Basu, S. (2013). Exploration and resource commitments in unequal partnerships: An examination of corporate venture capital investments. *Journal of Product Innovation Management, 30*(5), 916-936.

Wadhwa, A., Phelps, C., & Kotha, S. (2016). Corporate venture capital portfolios and firm innovation. *Journal of Business Venturing, 31*(1), 95-112.

Wagner, S. M. (2012). Tapping supplier innovation. *Journal of Supply Chain Management, 48*(2), 37-52.

Wagner, S. M., & Bode, C. (2011). A credit risk modelling approach to assess supplier default risk. In B. Hu, K. Morasch, S. Pickl, & M. Siegle (Eds.), *Operations Research Proceedings 2010* (pp. 471-476). Berlin, Heidelberg: Springer

Wagner, S. M., & Bode, C. (2014). Supplier relationship-specific investments and the role of safeguards for supplier innovation sharing. *Journal of Operations Management, 32*(3), 65-78.

Ward, T. B. (2004). Cognition, creativity, and entrepreneurship. *Journal of Business Venturing, 19*(2), 173-188.

Weiblen, T., & Chesbrough, H. W. (2015). Engaging with startups to enhance corporate innovation. *California Management Review, 57*(2), 66-90.

West, J., & Bogers, M. (2014). Leveraging external sources of innovation: A review of research on open innovation. *Journal of Product Innovation Management, 31*(4), 814-831.

Woehr, D. J., Loignon, A. C., Schmidt, P. B., Loughry, M. L., & Ohland, M. W. (2015). Justifying aggregation with consensus-based constructs: A review and examination of cutoff values for common aggregation indices. *Organizational Research Methods, 18*(4), 704-737.

Wolff, M. F. (1992). Scouting for technology. *Research-Technology Management, 35*(2), 10-12.

Wowak, K. D., Craighead, C. W., Ketchen, D. J., & Hult, G. T. M. (2016). Toward a "theoretical toolbox" for the supplier-enabled fuzzy front end of the new product development process. *Journal of Supply Chain Management, 52*(1), 66-81.

Wynstra, F., Van Weele, A., & Weggemann, M. (2001). Managing supplier involvement in product development: Three critical issues. *European Management Journal, 19*(2), 157-167.

Wynstra, F., Von Corswant, F., & Wetzels, M. (2010). In chains? An empirical study of antecedents of supplier product development activity in the automotive industry. *Journal of Product Innovation Management, 27*(5), 625-639.

Yang, H., Zheng, Y., & Zhao, X. (2014). Exploration or exploitation? Small firms' alliance strategies with large firms. *Strategic Management Journal, 35*(1), 146-157.

Yeniyurt, S., Henke Jr, J. W., & Yalcinkaya, G. (2014). A longitudinal analysis of supplier involvement in buyers' new product development: working relations, inter-dependence, co-innovation, and performance outcomes. *Journal of the Academy of Marketing Science, 42*(3), 291-308.

Yin, R. K. (2014). *Case study research: Design and methods* (Fifth ed.). London: SAGE.

Zahra, S. A. (1996). Technology strategy and new venture performance: A study of corporate-sponsored and independent biotechnology ventures. *Journal of Business Venturing, 11*(4), 289-321.

Zahra, S. A., Sapienza, H. J., & Davidsson, P. (2006). Entrepreneurship and dynamic capabilities: A review, model and research agenda. *Journal of Management Studies, 43*(4), 917-955.

Zander, U., & Kogut, B. (1995). Knowledge and the speed of the transfer and imitation of organizational capabilities: An empirical test. *Organization Science, 6*(1), 76-92.

Zaremba, B. W., Bode, C., & Wagner, S. M. (2016). Strategic and operational determinants of relationship outcomes with new venture suppliers. *Journal of Business Logistics, 37*(2), 152-167.

Zaremba, B. W., Bode, C., & Wagner, S. M. (2017). New venture partnering capability: An empirical investigation into how buying firms effectively leverage the potential of innovative new ventures. *Journal of Supply Chain Management, 53*(1), 41-64.

Zollo, M., Reuer, J. J., & Singh, H. (2002). Interorganizational routines and performance in strategic alliances. *Organization Science, 13*(6), 701-713.

Zollo, M., & Winter, S. G. (2002). Deliberate learning and the evolution of dynamic capabilities. *Organization Science, 13*(3), 339-351.

9. Appendix

9.1. Appendix Chapter 3

Interview guideline

Organization of search
- Point of contact for startups
- Definition of responsibilities
- Involvement of central business units, external business units, or external partners
- Roles of involved departments

Search strategies
- Search space considering local and distant knowledge provided by startups, e.g., cross-industry search
- Definition of needs and/or problems
- Search target: Type of startups, maturity and existing collaborations

Implementation of search
- Definition, implementation and maturity of search process
- Basis of search and search fields
- Existing search instruments and their application
- Support of search activities through external partners
- Application of search instruments: Timing, scope, recurrence, and responsibilities

Evaluation of search activities
- Successful and unsuccessful search for startups
- Evaluation of the defined search process

9.2. Appendix Chapter 4

Appendix Table 16: Scales

Scales	Factor loadings and Cronbach's alphas (α)
Search success	($α$ = 0.80)

Please indicate your opinion on the following statements referring to your firm's search success regarding the identification of startups. (1 = strongly disagree; 5 = strongly agree)

SE1:	We identify many startups for our portfolio.	0.730
SE2:	We identify sufficiently "good" and/or "right" startups for our portfolio.	0.761
SE3:	Our current startup portfolio will strengthen our competitive positioning.	0.808
SE4:	With our current startup portfolio we will be able to strongly increase our sales with new products within the next three years.	0.740
SE5:	At large, our current startup portfolio has a strong value generating potential.	0.714

Radical innovation capability	($α$ = 0.78)

How would you rate your company's capability to generate the following types of innovations in the products you have introduced in the last three years relative to your main competitors? (1 = much weaker than competition; 5 = much stronger than competition)

RAD1:	Innovations that make existing products obsolete	0.834
RAD2:	Innovations that fundamentally change existing products	0.853
RAD3:	Innovations that significantly enhance customers' product experiences	0.718
RAD4:	Innovations that require different ways of learning from customers	0.701

9.3. Appendix Chapter 5

Questionnaire

Introduction and background
- Previous experiences of entrepreneur within startups and corporate organizations
- Current financial and competitive situation of the firm
- Existing collaborations with corporations

No previous collaborations
- Offers made by corporations in the past
- Future collaborations intended
- Motivation, expectations and concerns regarding collaborations with corporations
- Preferred type of collaboration

Existing collaborations
- Type of corporate organization and collaborative agreement
- Development of collaboration over time
- Motivation, expectations and concerns regarding collaborations with corporations (ex ante)
- Benefits and drawbacks of collaborations (ex post)
- Comparison of different collaborations

Assets and risks regarding collaborations
- Importance of different risks and assets: Financial support, technological support, organizational support, corporation as a customer, reputation of corporation, risk of misappropriation, and risk of dependency

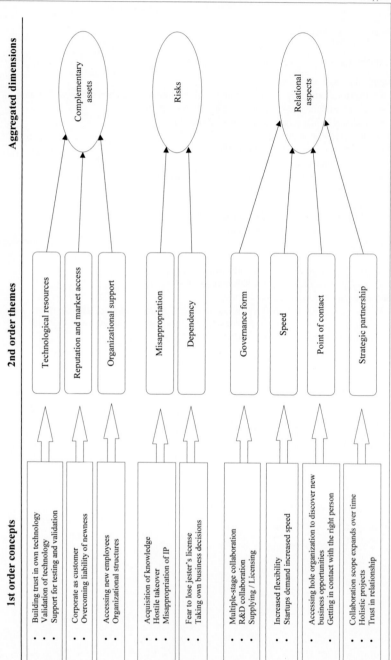

Appendix Figure 8: Data structure

Summary

"External knowledge sourcing from startups: An analysis of the pre-collaboration phase"

Digitalization forces firms in various traditional industries to respond to emerging technological developments and changes in their market environments more than ever. To face these challenges, firms need to constantly explore new technological paths and access knowledge beyond their boundaries. While prior research has primarily studied how firms access knowledge from established suppliers, startups have only recently evolved to an important external source of knowledge. This dissertation focuses on the identification of startups as knowledge providers for corporations and delivers new insights into the implications of corporate-startup collaborations.

This dissertation starts with the introduction of structured search approaches for the identification of startups, which are particularly important since the search for startups requires a radically different approach compared to distinguishing innovative firms within a corporation's network. A further analysis of search strategies for startups underlines that searching broadly and intensively increases the search success, i.e., the identification of adequate and value creating startups. In addition, one chapter of this thesis develops strategies on how corporations should act to become attractive partners for startups.

Second, two chapters of this work access the implications of sourcing knowledge from startups. It can be empirically proven that startups deliver ideas with higher novelty and customer benefit. However, startup ideas experience constraints concerning their implementation. In addition, the search for startups has positive effects on the organizational capabilities of the searching firm. By continuously screening startup ideas and interacting with entrepreneurial teams, corporations expand their radical innovation capabilities. Consequently, the findings provide evidence that the generation of knowledge is supported by including distant knowledge and interacting with new business partners such as startups.

Overall, this dissertation advances research on external knowledge sourcing. The findings underline the importance of investing time and resources in the search for startups as well as in building relationships based on equality. As a consequence, corporations benefit from truly innovative and novel ideas accompanied by evolving organizational capabilities that allow to develop and implement radically new product ideas.

Samenvatting (Summary in Dutch)

"Kennisuitwisseling met Startups: Een Analyse van de Fase van voor de Samenwerking"

Digitalisering dwingt bedrijven in de diverse traditionele bedrijfstakken om meer dan ooit te anticiperen op de opkomende technologische ontwikkelingen en de veranderingen in de markt. Om deze uitdagingen het hoofd te kunnen bieden, is het zaak voor bedrijven om voortdurend nieuwe technologische paden verkennen en om toegang te verkrijgen tot kennis buiten hun bereik. Terwijl eerder onderzoek zich voornamelijk richtte op hoe bedrijven toegang konden verkrijgen tot kennis van gevestigde leveranciers, worden startups pas recent gezien als een belangrijke externe bron van kennis. Dit proefschrift richt zich op de identificatie van startups als kennisleveranciers voor bedrijven en het levert daarbij nieuwe inzichten op ten aanzien van de gevolgen van samenwerkingsverbanden tussen bedrijven en startups.

Dit proefschrift vangt aan met de presentatie van gestructureerde zoekbenaderingen ten einde startups te identificeren. Deze identificatie is vooral van belang, omdat het onderscheiden van startups een totaal andere aanpak vereist dan het vinden van innovatieve bedrijven binnen de bestaande netwerken van ondernemingen. Een verdere analyse van zoekstrategieën voor startups toont aan dat de breedste en tevens meest diepgravende zoekmethode leidt tot de succesvolste identificatie van geschikte, waarde creërende startups. Daarnaast worden in een volgend hoofdstuk van dit proefschrift strategieën, over hoe bedrijven zouden moeten handelen om aantrekkelijke partners te worden voor startups, ontwikkeld.

De volgende twee hoofdstukken van deze studie zijn gewijd aan de implicaties van het verzamelen van kennis van startups. Er is empirisch bewijs dat ideeën van startups origineler zijn en een groter klantvoordeel opleveren. Echter, startup-ideeën hebben vaak te maken met beperkingen ten aanzien van de implementatie. Daarnaast blijkt de zoektocht naar startups een positief effect te hebben op de organisatorische capaciteiten van het zoekende bedrijf. Door de doorlopende screening van startup-ideeën en door de interactie met ondernemersteams, vergroten bedrijven hun radicale innovatiecapaciteiten. Bovendien, tonen de resultaten aan dat het genereren van kennis wordt gestimuleerd door de opname van ver verwijderde kennis en de interactie met nieuwe zakelijke partners, zoals startups.

Over het geheel genomen wordt in dit proefschrift onderzoek naar externe kennisbronnen verder ontwikkeld. De bevindingen onderstrepen het belang van het investeren van tijd en middelen bij het zoeken naar startups en bij het opbouwen van gelijkwaardige relaties. Als gevolg daarvan profiteren bedrijven van werkelijk innovatieve en nieuwe ideeën, die daarbij vergezeld gaan van veranderende organisatorische capaciteiten, die het mogelijk maken om radicaal nieuwe productideeën te ontwikkelen en te implementeren.

Acknowledgements

Although in the end only a single name appears on the cover, writing a dissertation takes more than the effort and passion of an individual. It takes the support, guidance, and companionship of many people.

First, I thank my supervisors Prof. Holger Schiele and Dr. Rainer Harms for their advice, support, and gentle pressure to advance the publications, to eventually finalize my dissertation and to achieve the defined goals. Thank you for showing me the big picture and guiding my way. I would also like to thank the members of my promotion committee, Prof. Fred van Houten, Prof. Celeste Wilderom, Prof. Jukka Hallikas, Prof. Christoph Ihl, and Dr. Louise Knight, for their valuable comments on this dissertation.

Second, I want to thank my industry partner AUDI AG for providing the opportunity to undertake this Ph.D. project. Especially, I would like to express my appreciation and thanks to my mentors Dr. Peter Faust, Dr. Hanno Brenner, and Til Fabio Schäfer. Thank you for providing the necessary perspective of practitioners whenever needed as well as for enabling the collection of data and supporting the participation in relevant academic conferences. In addition, I thank Prof. Christoph Bode, Prof. Ulli Arnold, and Dr. Frank Czymmek for many fruitful discussions during our meetings at the Autouni in Wolfsburg.

Moreover, I want to thank my co-workers at Audi and at the University of Twente. This work would not have been possible without your support – thank you for making my time as a doctoral student a great experience. In particular, I am thankful for getting the chance to collaborate with Felix and Vincent on parts of this dissertation. Felix, you have been a great sparring partner during the last three years – Danke! Klaas and Frederik, thank you for helping me with the final steps towards my defense.

I also want to thank Prof. Stefano Brusoni and Prof. Riitta Katila for taking the time to discuss my research and for showing me how the academic society collaborates across boarders without any formal agreements. Stefano, I am thankful for your support and advice during the most difficult times of this Ph.D.

Finally, I am deeply grateful to my family and friends who made all this possible by supporting and encouraging me along my way.